FOCUS ON GRAMMAR

Arbeitsbuch zur Wiederholung zentraler grammatischer Strukturen

NEW EDITION

von Willibald Bliemel und Brian McCredie

Vorwort

Focus on Grammar ist ein Arbeitsbuch zum Wiederholen und Festigen zentraler grammatischer Strukturen, die in der Sekundarstufe 1 behandelt wurden. *Focus on Grammar* ist ein wichtiges Hilfsmittel – bei der Arbeit im Klassenverband aber auch im Selbststudium.

Was ist neu?

- Grammatikarbeit mit neuen interessanten Themen: Das Spektrum reicht von *computers* to *doping in sport* bis zu *fair trade* und *multicultural societies*.

- Ein Schwerpunkt liegt auf den besonderen Problemen deutschsprachiger Lerner (*typical errors*, *false friends*, *spelling*). Nach jeder fünften Unit können die Lernenden ihren Leistungsstand überprüfen.

- Das Arbeitsbuch erscheint in Vierfarbendruck, der zusammen mit der Bebilderung und dem gefälligem Layout die Lernenden zusätzlich motivieren soll.

- Das Arbeitsbuch kann in zwei Ausgaben erworben werden: Arbeitsbuch ohne CD-ROM und Arbeitsbuch mit CD-ROM. Auf der CD-ROM befinden sich interaktive Übungen, die von den Lernenden direkt am Computer oder Laptop geübt und überprüft werden können. Die Übungen beziehen sich auf die Grammatik- und Themenschwerpunkte der Sektionen im Arbeitsbuch.

Verwendungsmöglichkeiten

Aufgrund seiner didaktischen Anlage kann *Focus on Grammar* bis zur Klasse 10, als Vorbereitung für den Realschulabschluss, für die Jahrgangsstufe 11 (Gymnasium; berufliches Gymnasium, Fachoberschule) zum Ausgleich unterschiedlicher Kenntnisse und für die Erwachsenenbildung auf dem Niveau B1 des Europäischen Referenzrahmens eingesetzt werden.

Aufbau

Das Arbeitsbuch ist in 20 Grammatiksektionen mit dazugehörenden themengebundenen Übungen gegliedert. In vier weiteren *Focus on ...* Sektionen werden spezielle Probleme deutschsprachiger Lernender aufgegriffen. In vier eingeschobenen Tests können die Lernenden ihre Kenntnisse überprüfen. Es folgen noch eine Liste der wichtigsten unregelmäßigen Verben, eine Zeitentabelle der englischen Zeitformen sowie eine Liste der wichtigsten englischen Grammatikbegriffe, die auf Deutsch erklärt werden und mit einem Beispielsatz versehen sind.

Lösungen

Die eingelegten Lösungen dienen insbesondere denjenigen zur Kontrolle, die *Focus on Grammar* im Selbststudium durcharbeiten. Die Richtigkeit der Bearbeitung von den CD-ROM Übungen kann direkt am Computer überprüft werden.

Wir wünschen allen Lernenden viel Freude bei der Arbeit mit *Focus on Grammar* und viel Erfolg!

Die Autoren und die Redaktion

Contents

Section	Grammar topic	Page
1	Adjectives	4
2	Adverbs	6
3	Position of adverbs	8
4	Quantifiers A: some, any, every, each, etc.	10
5	Quantifiers B: a lot of, much, many, few, etc.	12
Focus on …	Prepositional verbs	14
Test 1		15
6	Present tenses: simple present and present continuous	16
7	Past tenses A: simple past, past perfect and continuous forms	18
8	Past tenses B: present perfect and present perfect continuous	22
9	The future	26
10	The passive	30
Focus on …	False friends and other problems	32
Test 2		35
11	Reported speech	36
12	Modal auxiliaries A: can, be able to, be allowed to, may	38
13	Modal auxiliaries B: must, have to, should, ought, etc.	40
14	If-clauses	42
15	Relative clauses	44
Focus on …	Spelling A	46
Test 3		47
16	The participle	48
17	Forms of 'lassen': let, allow, permit, etc.	50
18	Gerund	52
19	Gerund and infinitive	54
20	Question tags	56
Focus on …	Spelling B	57
Test 4		60
	Phrasal verbs	61
	Grammar terminology	62
	Table of tenses	63
	Irregular verbs	64

1 Adjectives

1. The hotel was **lovely** with **friendly** staff.
2. Some 5-star hotels are **(not) as good as** some 4-star ones.
3. The weather in the west of Cyprus is often **warmer than** in the east.
4. Rooms on the upper floors of a hotel are **more attractive than** rooms on the lower floors because they have a better view.
5. Cyprus is one of the **most interesting** places I have ever been to.
6. Greek food tastes **delicious**.

- Die meisten Adjektive stehen nach einer Form von *be* oder vor einem Substantiv **(1)**.
- Die wichtigsten Vergleiche sind:
  (just) as … as = (genau) so …wie **(2)**
  not as … as = nicht so … wie **(2)**
  -er … than = -er als … **(3)**
  more … than = -er als … **(4)**

Steigerung von Adjektiven

- Kurze, einsilbige Adjektive werden mit *-er/-est* gesteigert:
  quick – quicker – quickest
- Ausnahmen: *good – better – best*
  bad – worse – worst
- Zweisilbige Adjektive, die auf *-y* enden, werden mit *-(i)er/-(i)est* gesteigert:
  happy – happier – happiest
- Andere zweisilbige Adjektive (nicht auf *-y*) und lange Adjektive (drei und mehr Silben) **(4, 5)** werden mit *more/most* gesteigert:
  modern – more modern – most modern
- Das Adjektiv wird außerdem benutzt bei Verben, die einen Zustand beschreiben: *appear, feel, look, smell, sound, taste* **(6)** sowie bei Verben, die dem deutschen „werden" entsprechen: *become, get*.

Watch out!

Adjektive beziehen sich normalerweise auf Nomen, während Adverbien (siehe dazu Seite 6) sich meistens auf Verben beziehen.

Holiday destinations

Tour operators try to describe holiday destinations as attractively as possible in their travel brochures to encourage you to book a trip there with them. Here is part of a travel brochure about Cyprus.

CYPRUS

A GREEK ISLAND PARADISE

The north of the island with its golden beaches and brilliant weather is generally considered to be the best and most beautiful part of the island. The Kyrenia harbour is one of many unforgettable sights waiting for you on your holiday. You will enjoy spectacular views and explore some of the most incredible historical and cultural sites. The lively town has over 300 restaurants and tavernas, serving a wide selection of local and international dishes. For the more adventurous travellers, there is also an excellent choice of activities such as horse riding, paragliding and water sports like scuba diving. The natural friendliness of the people and the island's pleasant climate will stay in your memory for years to come.

1a There are 18 adjectives in the text. Underline them.

1b There are three superlative forms and one comparative form. What are they?

_____ _____ _____

_____

2 Fill in the comparative and superlative forms of the adjectives.

1. good _____ _____
2. incredible _____ _____
3. beautiful _____ _____
4. quiet _____ _____
5. wide _____ _____
6. pleasant _____ _____
7. bad _____ _____
8. lively _____ _____

3 *Adjective or adverb? Cross out the incorrect form.*

1. Our travel company *consistent / consistently* wins travel awards.
2. Being a *full / fully* independent and *private / privately* owned tour operator, we do not depend on a *particular / particularly* airline.
3. Our all *inclusive / inclusively* holidays are of a higher standard than holidays *normal / normally* offered by our competitors.
4. Upon arrival at the airport you will be greeted by one of our *good / well* dressed *local / locally* representatives.
5. All of our staff visit the *different / differently* holiday sites *regular / regularly* as part of their training.
6. Online booking is *extreme / extremely* easy *easily* and *full / fully* secure.

4 *Comparing hotels: Fill in the missing parts of the comparisons below.*

Park Hotel *** double room $100 5 miles from centre 50 rooms	Black Inn ** double room $110 10 miles from centre 70 rooms	Hilton Hotel **** double room $140 walking distance to centre 100 rooms

1. (comfortable) According to the number of stars, the Park Hotel is _____ the Black Inn but the Hilton Hotel is _____ of the three.
2. (expensive) The Park Hotel isn't _____ the Black Inn and the Black Inn is less _____ the Hilton Hotel.
3. (near) The Hilton Hotel is the _____ hotel to the city centre. The Park Hotel is _____ to the city _____ the Black Inn.
4. (big) The Black Inn is _____ the Park Hotel but it isn't _____ the Hilton Hotel. The Hilton Hotel has got the (many) _____ rooms.

5 *Fill in the right adjective form of the nouns in brackets to find the answer to sentence 10. Then circle the right comparison words in the sentences.*

1. (width) Our hotel room in Cyprus is longer and … *as / than* the one we had last year.
2. (warmth) The water isn't as … *as / than* the temperature outside.
3. (publicity) There are a lot of private hotel beaches but there are also some … beaches.
4. (loveliness) We had a … view from our hotel room.
5. (attraction) Our hotel lobby is more … *as / than* the one next door.
6. (heat) The weather this year is the … we have ever had.
7. (easiness) – Why don't you book your holidays on the internet?
   – Well, that's … said *than / as* done. I haven't got a computer.
8. (normality) It's … to eat dinner late in Cyprus.
9. (greatness) – What about going to the beach?
   – Sure. That sounds … .
10. In my opinion, getting to know the culture of the country is more … *as / than* lying on the beach all day.

6 *Translate these sentences.*

1. Das Hilton Hotel ist das größte und modernste Hotel in der Stadt.
2. Der Wein riecht und schmeckt gut.
3. Urlaub in England ist teurer als Urlaub in Deutschland.
4. Das Wetter in Spanien war schlechter als zu Hause.
5. Urlaub in einem Hotel ist nicht so abenteuerlich wie Urlaub in einem Zelt.

2 Adverbs

1 Most navigation systems work **reliably** nowadays.
2 This system uses **extremely** expensive software.
3 It works **surprisingly well** for an inexpensive system.
4 **Unfortunately**, it has only got a small screen.

- Das Adverb bestimmt Verben (1), Adjektive (2), Adverbien (3) und ganze Sätze (4).
- Die Bildung von Adverbien erfolgt meist durch Anhängen von -ly an das Adjektiv (1–4).
- Das Adverb zu *good* ist *well* (3).
- Adverbien mit zwei Formen:
  Einige Adverbien haben neben der auf -ly endenden Form eine zweite Form, die wie ein Adjektiv aussieht. Die beiden Formen unterscheiden sich in der Bedeutung.
  *Installing the navigation system was **hard** work.*
  *He has **hardly** ever worked **so hard**.*

Adjektiv / Adverb		weitere vom Adverb abgeleitete Form	
close	nahe	closely (watch)	genau (beobachten)
deep	tief	deeply	zutiefst
fair	fair	fairly	ziemlich
hard	schwer	hardly	kaum
high	hoch	highly	höchst
late	spät	lately	vor kurzem, in letzter Zeit
most	am meisten	mostly	meistens
near	nahe (heran)	nearly	beinahe, fast
wide	weit (auf)	widely (known)	allgemein (bekannt)

- Einsilbige Adverbien werden mit -er und -est gesteigert:
  fast – faster – fastest
- Ausnahme: *well – better – best*

- Adverbien mit -ly werden mit *more* und *most* gesteigert:
  seriously – more seriously – most seriously
- Ausnahme: *badly – worse – worst*

Watch out!

Adjektive beziehen sich auf Nomen (siehe dazu Seite 4); Adverbien auf Verben, Adjektive, andere Adverbien oder auf einen ganzen Satz.

Customer satisfaction

Here are some customer comments on a navigation system's website.

User	Topic
carl	I definitely think this is one of the best GPS [*general positioning system*] devices available.
joe	It works brilliantly – it tells you the names of the roads and leads you exactly to where you want to go. It also showed me the distance to my destination accurately.
mike	Amazingly, it even gives information about traffic accidents or road works and then calculates a new route. It also quickly recognizes when you choose to go a different way. You really don't have to read the manual [*Bedienungsanleitung*], you can work it out intuitively.
gina	It navigates outstandingly well. I would thoroughly recommend it.

1a Underline all the adverbs and draw an arrow to the words they refer to.

1b One adverb refers to a second adverb. Which is it?
_____

1c One adverb refers to a whole sentence. Which is it?
_____

2 Write down the comparative/superlative forms of the adverbs, as well as their corresponding adjectives.

	adverb	comparative	superlative	adjective
1			most accurately	
2		worse		
3				easy
4				angry
5		better		
6	fast			
7	expensively			
8	hard			

3 Fill in the right forms of the adverbs in this negative consumer review.

I really wanted it to work _____ (good)¹ for me but all it has _____ (actual)² done is cause a lot of headaches. I _____ (serious)³ doubt that the software is up-to-date as it doesn't recognize the address of the train station I _____ (usual)⁴ travel to. Also, the device works much more _____ (slow)⁵ than most other ones at the same price level. It picks up signals really _____ (bad)⁶ and I can follow directions on my old road maps much more _____ (easy)⁷. _____ (unfortunate)⁸, using this device has wasted hours of my valuable time. So I'm returning it.

4 Adjective or adverb? Circle the right form.

The TV has a *fantastic / fantastically*¹ picture. The screen is *extreme / extremely*² bright and the image quality is *excellent / excellently*³. However, I have *unfortunate / unfortunately*⁴ found a defect that *serious / seriously*⁵ bothers me. There is a small spot on the bottom right-hand corner which is *definite / definitely*⁶ noticeable when *light / lightly*⁷ colours are shown on the screen. There are also some *dead / deadly*⁸ pixels which are *especial / especially*⁹ annoying. However, the TV has been a *good / well*¹⁰ investment overall.

5 Make comparative sentences. There are two ways.
New cars / run / economic / old cars.
New cars run more economically than old cars.
Old cars do not run as economically as new cars.

1 Expensive navigation systems / work / accurate / cheap navigation systems

_____
_____

2 The Transrapid / run / fast / high speed trains

_____
_____

3 Most young people / understand / technology / good / old people

_____
_____

6 Complete the sentences by putting the words in brackets in the right order. One of the words must be changed into an adverb.

1 (car / built / very good / a) We won't have to buy a new one for a long time because it is
a very well-built car.

2 (classical / camera / a / designed) The latest model is
_____

3 (user-friendly / extreme / software) The new computer uses
_____

4 (a / price / surprising / low) She bought her stereo at
_____

5 (disappointing / a / small / screen) The TV has
_____

7 Look at the special forms of the adjectives and adverbs in the grammar column and fill them in to the puzzle.

[Crossword puzzle with 1 across = WIDELY]

1 HD TVs are … available nowadays.
2 It is never too … to learn something new.
3 The software is updated … every year.
4 There is a … selection of navigation systems available.
5 The instruction manual was complicated – I … understood it.
6 It is … young people who work in the IT business.
7 Make sure you read the instructions … before using the navigation system.
8 A lot of new mobile phones have appeared in the shops … but they are all too expensive for me.
9 I think it is … likely that all cars will have a navigation system in the near future.
10 She drives very … – she's always looking at her map and not at the road.

3 Position of adverbs

A Häufigkeitsadverbien

1 Mary **often** drinks at the weekend.
2 Her boyfriend has **often** got drunk at the disco.
3 Alcohol is **often** the reason for violence.
4 Some teenagers drink **daily**.

● **Häufigkeitsadverbien der unbestimmten Zeit** stehen vor dem ersten Hauptverb* **(1)**, nach dem ersten Hilfsverb **(2)**, und nach *to be* **(3)**. Zu ihnen gehören: *already, always, ever, frequently, just* [gerade, eben], *mostly, never, normally, often, rarely, regularly, sometimes, seldom, soon, usually*.

● **Häufigkeitsadverbien der bestimmten Zeit** stehen meistens am Satzende, z.B. *annually, daily, monthly, once, twice, weekly, yearly* **(4)**. Dies gilt auch für *a lot, before, very much, yet*.

*Ein Hauptverb kann alleine im Satz auftreten; ein Hilfsverb steht nie ohne ein zweites Verb und fügt dem Satz eine weitere Bedeutung bei.

B Andere Adverbien

1 My friends often go drinking **in the pub**.
2 Alcohol **definitely** makes Bill aggressive.
3 The police managed the situation **well**.

● **Adverbialbestimmungen des Ortes, der Zeit und der Art und Weise** (*October 25th, next month, in an agressive manner, at the disco, at the cinema,* usw.) und Zusammensetzungen (*as soon as possible, most of the time, now and again,* usw.) stehen meistens am Satzende **(1)**.

● **Gradadverbien** können eine Aussage stärken oder abschwächen. Sie stehen an derselben Stelle im Satz wie die Häufigkeitsadverbien der unbestimmten Zeit **(2)**. Zu ihnen gehören: *almost, completely, definitely, even, hardly, nearly, only, particularly, quite, rather, scarcely, really, too*.

● **Adverbien der Art und Weise** stehen in der Regel nach dem Verb (+ Objekt) **(3)**. Zu ihnen gehören: *angrily, badly, carefully, easily, quickly, successfully, slowly, shyly, well*.

Watch out!

1 Folgende Adverbien stehen meistens am Satzanfang: *anyway* [immerhin, jedenfalls], *(un)fortunately, maybe, obviously, perhaps, probably, yet* [dennoch].
2 Art und Weise vor Ort vor Zeit: *Street workers have solved problems **successfully in our town this year**.*

Help – I'm a teenage alcoholic!

Teenagers drink far too much nowadays. The small town of Tenby in south Wales is typical and has almost more pubs per square mile than anywhere in Britain.

1 *Rewrite the sentence with the adverb in brackets in the best position.*

1 Tenby has a population of 5,000 people. (normally)
Tenby normally has a population of 5,000 people.

2 But this number rises to about 50,000. (every summer)
_____

3 Young people go there to enjoy the pubs and parties. (from June to August)
_____

4 The first teenage alcoholics appeared a few years ago. (in Tenby)
_____

5 Most pub owners don't allow young people to drink in their pub. (obviously)
_____

6 It does happen now and again. (unfortunately)
_____

7 The police close pubs where young people are served alcohol. (sometimes)
_____

8 So any teenagers who are under 18 years old are not served. (mostly)
_____

9 Young people drink too much because of peer pressure [*Gruppendruck*]. (usually)
_____

10 Binge drinking [*‚Komasaufen'*] has become a huge problem in Britain. (already)
_____

2 *Complete these comments from young drinkers in Tenby. Put the adverbs in the best possible place.*

1. I don't think [ ] our town [ ] treats [*behandeln*] young people [a].   a well

2. Tenby [ ] depends [ ] on thousands of tourists and [ ] it [ ] is [ ] interested in a few local teenagers.
   a hardly   b completely

3. Society says [ ] young people [ ] should enjoy themselves [ ] [ ].
   a at the weekend   b in clubs and bars

4. The owner of the pub near us [ ] will [ ] serve [ ] us kids [ ] – when the tourists have gone.
   a in the winter   b only

5. [ ] It can [ ] [ ] be a problem even if you're not under-age. If [ ] you look young, you have to show [ ] ID [ ].
   a definitely   b in some bars

6. Bars are not just for getting drunk in, you know – my friends and I are [ ] happy to [ ] sit and drink [ ] [ ].
   a in a corner   b peacefully

7. I'd say that the police [ ] haven't [ ] managed [ ] the situation [ ] [ ] [ ].
   a in Tenby   b sensibly   c so far

8. There are lots of bars [ ] where they [ ] check [ ] your ID [ ].
   a at the door

9. My boyfriend and his friends [ ] are [ ] drunk [ ].
   a by ten o'clock at night   b generally

3 *Right [✓] or wrong [✗]? Read Anja's interview with the BBC and correct her word order. In three cases the word order is already correct.*

BBC Anja, you've lived in Oxford for three months and we'd like to hear what you think about teenage drinking.

Anja Well, I think it **already** has become very serious [✗]¹. But **also** we Germans have an increasingly big problem with drinking **in some large towns** [ ]². **Fortunately**, it's not so easy for young people to buy alcohol here, but they don't check **generally** your ID **in the evening at the pub** [ ]³.

BBC Have you noticed a lot of violence among drunk teenagers?

Anja Well, it's **scarcely** possible not to bump into drunk teenagers **after midnight in the town centre** [ ]⁴. And, yes, **frequently** I have seen violence [ ]⁵. You know, when some people are drunk they get aggressive quickly and they stay **often** like that **for hours and hours** [ ]⁶.

BBC And what about you? Have you ever become aggressive because of alcohol, Anja?

Anja Me? No, but I have noticed that spirits **almost always** seem to cause aggression [ ]⁷.

BBC And was there much drinking at your school in Germany?

Anja Not at school, but some of my school friends drink **regularly** a lot of beer **at the local disco on Fridays and Saturdays** [ ]⁸. **Perhaps** it's too late to do anything to help some young people [ ]⁹. They will **maybe** become real alcoholics [ ]¹⁰.

Now look at the wrong sentences again and decide why they are wrong. Use the grammar box to help you.

4 *Translate these sentences using the best possible word order.*

1. Zu viel Alkohol kann das Gehirn [*brain*] komplett zerstören.

2. Das Problem ist kaum lösbar [*solvable*].

3. Leider trinken viele Teenager regelmäßig Spirituosen.

4. Am Wochenende saufen auch junge Mädchen in Pubs und Discos.

5. Jugendliche, die häufig besoffen sind, sind meistens aggressiv.

6. Alkohol ist immer wieder die Ursache [*cause*] von Gewalt auf den Straßen.

7. In Großbritannien sah man vor einigen Jahren selten asoziales Verhalten [*anti-social behaviour*].

8. Die Situation ist in einigen Städten generell außer Kontrolle geraten [*to get out of control*].

4 Quantifiers A

some – any – every – each – none – nobody

1. **Some** people have never known happiness.
2. Would you like **some** tips about how to be happy?
3. I haven't got **any** idea what happiness is.
4. Do you have **any** idea why so many people are unhappy?
5. **Every** expert has an explanation but **each** person is different.
6. **Any** definition of happiness is useful, but **none** covers all the aspects.
7. Perhaps **nobody** will ever be able to define what happiness is.

- *Some* und die Ableitungen (*somebody, something,* usw.) benutzt man vorwiegend in bejahenden Sätzen **(1)**, aber auch in Bitten und Angeboten bzw. Fragen, auf die man eine Zustimmung erwartet **(2)**.
- *Any* und die Ableitungen (*anybody, anything,* usw.) benutzt man vorwiegend in verneinenden Sätzen **(3)** und Fragen **(4)**. *Any* in einem bejahenden Satz heißt „jede/r/s beliebige" **(6)**.
- Man benutzt *every* für eine unbestimmte Anzahl von Dingen oder Personen und *each* für jede/s einzelne Person oder Ding in einer Gruppe **(5)**. (Außerdem wird *every* häufig bei Zeitangaben benutzt – *every two months, every Easter, every three weeks,* usw.)
- *None* wird nominal verwendet und heißt „keine/r/s" **(6)**; *nobody* bedeutet „niemand" **(7)**.

Watch out!

1. jemand von (uns) = *one of (us), somebody*
   niemand von (uns) = *none of (us), nobody*
2. Die Kombinationen *somebody of* und *nobody of* existieren im Englischen nicht (das gleiche gilt für *anybody of / everybody of*).
3. Im Englischen steht nach *everybody* das Verb im Singular!

Happy? – Who is or isn't, and why (1)

On a recent TV programme, 'Happiness UK', Professor Jenny Austin talked about what Britons need to be happier. Here is the start of the interview.

1 *Some or any? Circle the best solution.*

Reporter Professor Austin, I'd like to begin with *some / any*¹ questions about happiness in Britain. The newspapers nowadays are always full of bad news. Do we actually have *some / any*² reason to feel happy?

Jenny Well, there are *some / any*³ obvious reasons to be happy. I mean, no one is starving [verhungern] to death on our city streets, for example. That's a big contrast to *some / any*⁴ African nations. And there aren't *some / any*⁵ kids today who don't really have the chance of an education. Those are clearly *some / any*⁶ positive factors, I'd say.

Reporter True, but *some / any*⁷ people still aren't happy. Do you see *some / any*⁸ way at all to change things?

Jenny Oh, I don't have *some / any*⁹ magic solutions, but, you know, *some / any*¹⁰ sociologists think we should work less. And *some / any*¹¹ experts suggest we need to think about money less.

Reporter That sounds like a good idea, but surely we need *some / any*¹² money in the bank because, without it, we won't have *some / any*¹³ chance of success …

How happy are you?

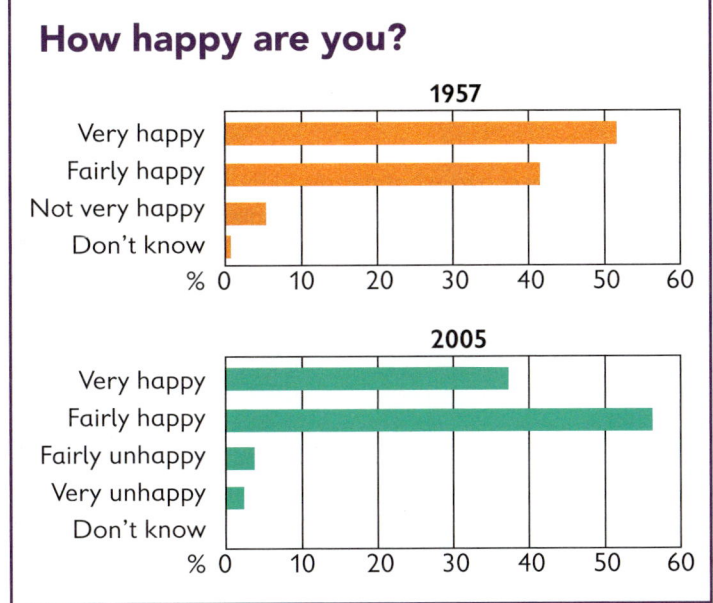

2 Look at the graphs above and complete the sentences using some, somebody, something, somewhere, any, anybody, anything or anywhere.

1 In 1957 _____ sections of the British population – 52% to be exact – felt 'very happy', _____ which is hard to imagine today when only 36% say the same.

2 The results show that _____ can be unhappy, no matter who they are. Maybe we can't do _____ to change that.

3 A lack of happiness also affects Americans and other rich nations. People don't seem to be 100% happy _____ .

4 There must be _____ who is completely happy with their life _____ in the world.

5 Is there _____ chance that people will be happier in the next survey?

3 Each or every? Circle the best solution.

1 *Each / Every* of the people interviewed for the study was at least 15 years old.

2 The organization carries out surveys like this *each / every* year, normally *each / every* January.

3 *Each / every* year hundreds of people answer questions for the survey.

4 Sociologists regularly organize surveys in *each / every* of the EU states.

5 Is *each / every* European content?

4 Beverly Phillips has written a book about happiness. Complete the sentences using each, every, everybody, everything or everywhere.

Beverly Phillips asked _____ [1] reader the same question: Should the government offer _____ [2] maximum wealth or maximum happiness? Beverly says she searched _____ [3] for people who were more interested in wealth, but in fact well over 80% of those interviewed said that _____ [4] they owned was less important than being happy. They thought that happiness was a basic human right [Menschenrecht] for _____ [5]. But Ms Phillips says she has _____ [6] reason to believe that politicians can't do much to help. 48% of the people interviewed felt that good relationships were important for _____ [7], no matter who they are. Happy people have close friends and good relationships.

5 Complete the speech bubbles using nobody, none, nothing or nowhere.

5 Quantifiers B

a lot of / lots of – much – many – most
(a) few – fewer – less – (a) little

1 They asked me **a lot of** questions about happiness. The survey took **a lot of** time.
2 How **many** people feel good about themselves all the time?
3 I don't have **much** patience with unhappy people.
4 **Most** people get depressed occasionally.
5 **Most of the** people we know are quite happy.
6 **Few** [*wenig/e/*] human beings are permanently happy. **A few** [*ein paar / einige*] are always unhappy though and it can be **a little** [*ein wenig / etwas*] difficult to help a person like that.

- *A lot of* benutzt man sowohl bei zählbaren Substantiven wie auch bei nichtzählbaren **(1)** (*lots of* ist weniger formell).
- *Many*, *(a) few* benutzt man bei zählbaren Begriffen **(2, 6)**; *much*, *(a) little* bei nichtzählbaren **(3, 6)**. (Dies gilt natürlich auch für *fewer* und *less* als Steigerungsformen der Pronomen *(a) few*, *(a) little*.)
- *Much/many* und *a lot of/lots of* sind oft austauschbar. *A lot of/lots of* werden aber häufig in bejahenden Sätzen verwendet.
- *Most* steht ohne Artikel, wenn es „fast alle / der größere Teil" in einem allgemeinen Sinn verwendet wird **(4)**; *most of the …* wird verwendet, wenn das folgende Substantiv, auf das es sich bezieht, sich auf etwas Bestimmtes bezieht **(5)**.

Watch out!

Vor der Mengenangabe *most …* steht **kein** Artikel. ~~The~~ Most people think money brings happiness.

Happy? – Who is or isn't, and why (2)

The table below shows what people in four English-speaking countries think would make people happier.

	Religion	Marriage	Shorter working week	Non-violent video games
UK	9%	69%	11%	3%
USA	66%	15%	83%	12%
Canada	21%	77%	96%	71%
Australia	58%	12%	76%	81%

1 *Use the information from the table to complete the sentences with a lot of / lots of, much, many, (a) few, fewer, less or (a) little.*

_____ ¹ people think marriage can make you happy, but very _____ ² Britons think that non-violent video games play a role in happiness. The shorter working week enjoys _____ ³ support in the UK, which is certainly _____ ⁴ surprising.

In Britain, religion has _____ ⁵ importance than it does anywhere else. In fact, there seems to be _____ ⁶ possibility of religion offering true happiness.

In Australia, there doesn't seem to be _____ ⁷ support for marriage. There is clearly _____ ⁸ interest in it than in Canada and Britain.

The reduced working week has _____ ⁹ fans 'down under', although _____ ¹⁰ people are in favour than in the States and a good deal _____ ¹¹ than in Canada.

How _____ ¹² nations would feel happier with a ban [*Verbot*] on violent video games? Well, not _____ ¹³ British citizens, who don't seem to have _____ ¹⁴ time for this. A ban there would probably have _____ ¹⁵ or no chance at all of support.

Maybe the only means to be happy – at least in _____ ¹⁶ societies such as Canada, the USA or Australia – is to spend _____ ¹⁷ hours at work. So: work _____ ¹⁸ and feel good?!

2 Read the text about a different way that dogs can help make people happy and translate the words in brackets. Sometimes there is more than one solution.

Adolescents are very often _____ (ein wenig)¹ – even very – unhappy and may have _____ (viele)² problems but _____ (wenige)³ close friends. In the small town of Midhurst in West Sussex, _____ (ein paar)⁴ dogs – mostly Labradors and golden retrievers at a centre called Canine Partners (CP) – are trying to make life _____ (weniger)⁵ difficult for young people. The dogs here are normally trained to help the disabled [Schwerbehinderte], whom _____ (die meisten)⁶ teenagers normally have _____ (wenig)⁷ contact with. For _____ (ein paar)⁸ weeks the youngsters get _____ (viele)⁹ possibilities to find happiness and discipline in their lives. They learn how to become dog trainers and see that, just like the dogs, there are _____ (ein paar)¹⁰ rules human beings must follow. And that gives the youngsters the help and balance they need. The first adolescents to take part in the programme all felt far _____ (weniger)¹¹ unbalanced after their time at CP and they all had far _____ (weniger)¹² problems keeping themselves happy and out of trouble.

3 Spot the problem and correct these sentences. Look at the grammar from parts A and B.

1 Nobody of us can be happy all the time.

2 Not everybody are able to define happiness.

3 This institute does a survey all two years or so.

4 I cannot imagine some method at all that might improve things for us.

5 Less kids appear to be happy in today's world.

6 The most youngsters need rules and guidelines to help them find a path to happiness.

7 How much of us here would be interested in going to the CP centre?

8 There seems to be a little hope of arranging a visit at the moment.

4 Translate these sentences using the grammar you have learned in parts A and B.

1 Keiner der Jugendlichen dachte, dass ein Labrador viel helfen würde.
2 Weniger Sorgen bedeuten, dass man weniger unglücklich ist.
3 Die meisten Frauen, die unglücklich sind, sind bis [up to] 30 oder 40 oft ein wenig deprimierter [more depressed] als Männer in demselben Alter [of the same age].
4 Viele ältere Menschen sind die meiste Zeit ganz glücklich.
5 Niemand von uns ist immer ausgeglichen, denn jeder hat gewisse negative Gefühle.
6 Jedes der Kids hat etwas aus dem CP-Programm gelernt.
7 Es kann jedem zu jeder Zeit passieren.
8 Irgendwo auf dieser Welt gibt es glückliche Menschen.

To make people happier, the Himalayan state of Bhutan banned advertising, the TV channel MTV, and plastic bags!

Focus on ... Prepositional verbs

Don't **laugh at** me; it's not funny.
Does this workbook **belong to** you?
Do you **believe in** life after death?
She **apologized for** her bad behaviour.

- *Prepositional verbs* bestehen aus Verb + Präposition (*at, to, by, in, for,* etc.). Im Gegensatz zu den *phrasal verbs* (siehe S. 61) werden bei den *prepositional verbs* Verb und Präposition nicht getrennt. Das Objekt, ob Nomen oder Pronomen, steht immer nach der Präposition, z.B. *laugh at somebody/something* = „über jemanden/etwas lachen". Lernen Sie deshalb immer die Wortfolge von Verb, Präposition und Objekt auswendig.

Quotations *[Zitate]*

Quotations and proverbs *[Sprichwörter]* have a similar function. You can use both in everyday communication if you want to stress or prove something you say. You can often find the right quotation or proverb to make your point *[ein Argument vorbringen]*. The following quotations and proverbs contain prepositional verbs.

1 *Underline the prepositional verbs and the object. Then write down the infinitive and the German translation. Use a dictionary if you need help.*

1 <u>Hope for</u> miracles *[Wunder]* but don't <u>rely on them</u>. (Yiddish proverb)

   hope for something = auf etwas hoffen
   rely on something = sich auf etwas verlassen

2 There is hope for any man who can look in a mirror and laugh at what he sees. (Anonymous)

_____ = _____
_____ = _____

3 People who can agree on what's funny can usually agree on other things too. (Anonymous)

_____ = _____

4 Happiness depends on ourselves. (Aristotle)

_____ = _____

5 The future belongs to those who believe in the beauty of their dreams. (Eleanor Roosevelt)

_____ = _____
_____ = _____

6 Nobody can live on beauty, but they can die for it. (Proverb)

_____ = _____
_____ = _____

2 *Fill in the right prepositional verb from exercise 1.*

1 It was difficult to _____ where to go on holiday. We all wanted to go to different places.

2 Most people _____ a better life after death.

3 You can't _____ David. He never does what you ask him to.

4 It _____ the weather. If it's raining, we'll go to the cinema.

5 Does this book _____ you? It's not mine.

6 I need to eat meat sometimes. I can't _____ just fruit and vegetables.

3 *Match the prepositional verb with its German translation.*

1	to talk to somebody	a	sich zu etwas entschließen
2	to think of something	b	an etwas denken
3	to talk about somebody	c	jemandem zuhören
4	to ask for something	d	jemanden suchen
5	to look for somebody	e	sich um etwas kümmern
6	to listen to somebody	f	auf etwas zielen
7	to refer to something	g	etwas anschauen
8	to take care of something	h	sich nach etwas sehnen
9	to long for something	i	mit jemandem reden
10	to aim at something	j	um etwas bitten
11	to look at something	k	sich auf etwas beziehen
12	to decide on something	l	über jemanden reden

   1 *i.* 2 ... 3 ... 4 ... 5 ... 6 ...
   7 ... 8 ... 9 ... 10 ... 11 ... 12 ...

Test 1

Adjectives and adverbs (▶ S.4, S.6)

1 *Cars*
Fill in the adjective or adverb of the words in brackets.

1 The Legus is a very _____ (comfortable) car.
2 It goes very _____ (fast) and the engine is _____ (quiet).
3 You can _____ (hard) hear the radio in some cars because they have _____ (terrible) _____ (loud) engines.
4 You can buy some new cars now for a _____ (surprising) _____ (low) price.

2 *Comparing people*
Finish the sentences. You will need to use the right forms of the adjective in brackets.

Both Jenny and Carla speak French, but Carla speaks it almost fluently. Sarah speaks French like a native speaker. (good at)

1 Carla is _____ _____ Jenny.
2 Jenny isn't _____ Carla.
3 Sarah is _____ .

Tony, George and Peter started their careers in the same company. George has been promoted once. Tony has been promoted twice. Peter is now the boss. (successful)

4 George is _____.
5 Tony isn't _____.
6 Peter is the _____ of the three men.

Word order (▶ S.8)

3 *The stressful job of a nurse*
Make sentences with these words. Choose the best possible word order.

1 Sheila / has to / often / in the hospital / at night / work
_____
_____

2 The patients / a hard time / give / her / sometimes
_____
_____

3 Yesterday / called her to come to his room / after midnight / three times / a patient
_____
_____

4 She / after a night shift / usually / at 6 a.m. / goes home
_____
_____

5 Her husband / at dinner / often only / her / sees
_____
_____

Quantifiers (▶ S.10, S.12)

4 *Famous people*
Complete the sentences with words from the box.

> any • anybody • anywhere •
> each • every • everything •
> nowhere • some • somebody

1 Nowadays with TV shows like Big Brother _____ can become famous.
2 Many famous people can't go _____ without being recognized. _____ time they go out, _____ recognizes them.
3 _____ celebrities like being recognized; others complain that they don't have _____ privacy. They feel there is _____ to hide.
4 Newspapers report about famous people _____ day but don't believe _____ they say.

5 *A successful woman's problems*
Circle the correct words.

1 Jennifer has got *many / much* friends, but she hasn't got *many / much* real friends.
2 She is very rich and earns *a lot of / many* money but she doesn't have *much / many* time to enjoy and spend it.
3 Now that she has got a promotion she has even *less / little* time for her hobbies than she used to have.
4 There are only very *few / little* people in the company who work as hard as Jennifer.
5 She would like to work *less / fewer* hours a week.

15

6 Present tenses

simple present – present continuous

	Bejahung	Verneinung
1	Marion **likes** her family.	She **doesn't like** fast food.
2	Her host mum **cooks** well.	She **doesn't cook** every day.
3	Marion and Avril usually **start** school at 8 a.m.	They normally **don't leave** before 3 p.m.
4	She **is writing** a letter at the moment.	She **isn't listening** to her iPod now.

- Das *simple present* wird benutzt für feststehende Tatsachen **(1)**, gewohnheitsmäßige oder regelmäßige Handlungen **(2, 3)**. Signalwörter sind *always*, *usually*, *often*, *sometimes*, *never*.
- Das *present continuous* wird benutzt für etwas, was gerade abläuft oder von begrenzter Dauer ist **(4)**. Signalwörter sind *now*, *at the moment*, *just*.
- Beachten Sie, dass beim *simple present* in der 3. Person Einzahl ein *s* an das Verb angehängt wird **(1, 2)**.
- Verben im *simple present* werden mit *do not* oder *does not* verneint **(1–3)**.
- **Remember**:

simple present	present continuous
always, usually, often, sometimes, never	now, at the moment, just

Fragen

1 **Do** exchange students **have** to pay for school?
2 Where **does** Marion **live**?
3 Who **shares** the room with her?
4 What **can** she do to improve her English?
5 **Are** Marion and her host sister **listening** to music at the moment?

- Fragen im *simple present* werden mit *do* oder *does* umschrieben **(1-2)**. Ausnahmen sind Fragen, die nach dem Subjekt eines Satzes fragen **(3)** oder Fragen, in denen eine Form von *be*, *have got*, *must*, *can* … vorkommt **(4)**.
- Fragen im *present continuous* werden durch Umstellung von Hilfsverb (*am*, *is*, *are*) und Subjekt gebildet **(5)**.

Watch out!

1 Bei einem Vollverb in der 3. Person Einzahl: *He*, *she*, *it* das *s* muss mit.
2 Aus *do* wird in Frage und Verneinung *does*, aus *have* wird *has*.

The exchange student experience

Here is an email from a German exchange student in California. She is writing to her English pen friend.

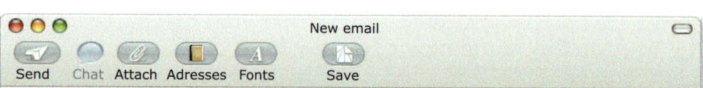

Dear Maria

Just a short update about what I'm doing here in Santa Anna High School. It's very different here. For example, there are about 70% Latinos in my school. It sometimes feels a bit strange but it doesn't really bother me. And everybody wants to talk to me because I come from Germany. They ask me all sorts of questions!

My host family is really friendly. My host mom knows the school basketball trainer and she's going to ask him if I can join the team! It'll be great fun! I share a room with Avril, my 17-year-old host sister. She's very nice and we get along with each other really well. Of course, I often miss my family, but I don't feel lonely. What I really miss is my mother's cooking. There's nothing quite like it.

Well, that's all for now. Hope to hear from you soon!

Love Marion

1a *Underline the simple present forms in the email. There is also one present continuous form. What is it?*

_____

1b *Why is this form used?*

   a It is happening now.   b It always happens.

2 *Circle the right verb form.*

1 Marion *share / shares* a room with Avril.
2 She *doesn't feel / doesn't feels* lonely.
3 She *miss / misses* her family.
4 She *like / likes* basketball.
5 She *doesn't phone / don't phone* home very often.

3 *Look at the email again and correct these sentences.*

1 There are not many Latinos in Marion's school.

_____

2 Most students don't want to talk to her.
_____

3 Marion and Avril don't share a room.
_____

4 Marion's host mum doesn't know the basketball trainer.
_____

5 Marion doesn't miss her family.
_____

6 Marion feels lonely.
_____

4 Ask questions with who or what.

1 Marion comes home from school at 3 o'clock.
_____ ?

2 She misses her mother's cooking.
_____ ?

3 Avril and Marion share the room.
_____ ?

4 Avril gets along with Marion very well.
_____ ?

5 Marion phones her mother every week.
_____ ?

5 Fill in the right present continuous forms of the verbs in the box.

> cook • do • leave • show • watch • write

Bob Hi Marion. It's Bob. What _____ you _____¹?

Marion Hi Bob. I _____² an email to my mum in Germany. What about you?

Bob Well, I _____³ TV. They _____⁴ some old *Friends* episodes tonight. But I've already seen them so do you want to go to the movies tonight? We could see that new film with Tom Richard.

Marion Well, my host mum _____⁵ dinner at the moment. But we could go afterwards. Do you want to come over for dinner before?

Bob Cool. That would be great. I _____ just _____⁶ now. I'll be there in ten minutes.

6 Complete the sentences with the right forms of the simple present or present continuous.

1 At 7.30 a.m. Marion usually _____ (listen) to her iPod on the bus which _____ (take) her to school. But today she _____ still _____ (sleep) and _____ (dream) about her family.

2 School always _____ (start) at 8 o'clock. But now it's 8 o'clock on Sunday morning and Marion _____ (get up).

3 At 10 o'clock she usually _____ (have) a maths lesson. But today she _____ (go) to church with her American family. They always _____ (go) to church on Sunday.

4 Marion always _____ (have) her lunch break at 12 o'clock. She usually _____ (eat) in the school cafeteria but she _____ (not like) the food there much. Today she _____ (have) lunch with her host family and she _____ (enjoy) it.

7 Match the questions with the right answers.

1	Do you have an iPod?	A	No, they're not. They think it's a great opportunity.
2	Are you having a party for your birthday?	B	No, she isn't. She doesn't have much time.
3	Do your host parents treat you well?	C	No, she doesn't. She doesn't have much time.
4	Are your parents sad about you being here?	D	No, I'm not. I can't afford one.
5	Is your host sister learning German?	E	Yes, they do. They're very nice.
6	Does your mother phone you often?	F	No, I don't. I can't afford one.

8 Translate these sentences.

1 Was macht er gerade? – Er schreibt eine Mail.
2 Wer bezahlt die Kosten für den Austausch?
3 Wie findet man eine gute amerikanische Schule?
4 Was interessiert deutsche Schüler in Amerika?
5 Mehr und mehr Austauschstudenten kommen nach Amerika.
6 Manche Schüler vertragen sich nicht mit ihren Gasteltern.

7 Past tenses A

simple past – past perfect – continuous forms

	Bejahung	Verneinung
1	Bill Gates and Paul Allen **founded** Microsoft.	They **didn't work** together for long.
2	They **were working** on the software **for weeks**.	At that time they **weren't sleeping** much.
3	After they **had finished** the new software, they sold it to the company.	They **hadn't thought** they could finish the new software so soon.
4	Bill Gates **had been studying** at Harvard for three years when he left.	He **hadn't been enjoying** his studies very much.

- Bei regelmäßigen Verben wird im *simple past* ein *-ed* an den Infinitiv des Verbs angehängt (1).
- Die Vergangenheitsformen der unregelmäßigen Verben befinden sich in der Liste auf Seite 64.
- In Verneinungen werden Vollverben mit *did not* umschrieben. Da *did* schon die Vergangenheit ausdrückt, steht das Verb im Infinitiv (1).
- „Signalwörter" für das *simple past* sind: *yesterday*, *last week*, *ago* und andere bestimmte Zeitangaben.

- Das *past continuous* wird gebildet aus *was/were* + *-ing*-Form. Es wird benutzt für Handlungen, die zu einem bestimmten Zeitpunkt in der Vergangenheit im Gange waren (2).

- Das *past perfect* wird gebildet aus *had* + *past participle* (entspricht der 3. Form des Verbs). Es zeigt an, dass etwas vor einem vergangenen Zeitpunkt abgeschlossen wurde. Es tritt häufig in Nebensätzen mit *when*, *as soon as* und *after* auf (3).

- Das *past perfect continuous* wird gebildet aus *had been* + *-ing*-Form. Es zeigt an, dass die Handlung in der Vorvergangenheit begann und bis zu einem bestimmten Zeitpunkt in der Vergangenheit andauerte (4).

1 **Did** Bill Gates **use** other programmers' ideas?
2 **When did** he **found** Microsoft?
3 **Who helped** him with BASIC?

- In Fragen im *simple past* werden Vollverben mit *did* umgeschrieben (1, 2).
- Beachten Sie, dass Fragen im *simple past* mit *who* oder *what* nicht mit *did* umschrieben werden (3).

Watch out!

Fragen und Verneinungen in der Vergangenheit werden nicht mit *did* umschrieben, wenn eine Form von *be*, *have got* oder *can* benutzt wird.

Computers

1a *Look at this text about the birth of Microsoft and fill in the simple past forms of the verbs in brackets.*

In January 1975 Paul Allen was reading a book in a book store when he _____ (see)[1] a picture of the Altair 8080 on the cover of a magazine. The Altair was a relatively small computer, not like the huge commercial computers that _____ (be)[2] already on the market. Paul _____ (buy)[3] the magazine and _____ (show)[4] it to his friend, Bill Gates. They _____ (recognize)[5] the Altair's potential for the home computer market straightaway. They also _____ (know)[6] that there was no software for the Altair yet. Bill _____ (call)[7] the company and _____ (tell)[8] them that they _____ (have)[9] a program for it. This wasn't true – they _____ (not even have)[10] an Altair! However, the company _____ (not know)[11] this and wanted to see their programming language. Bill and Paul _____ (develop)[12] BASIC on a university computer and, after eight weeks, it was time to demonstrate it on an Altair which they had never touched before! Surprisingly, the program _____ (work)[13] perfectly the first time. Bill _____ (leave)[14] his studies at Harvard and _____ (start)[15] a company called Micro – soft (a combination of micro and software) in 1976. It later _____ (become)[16] one word – Microsoft.

1b There is 1 past continuous form in the text. What is it?
_____

1c What is the right explanation for the use of this tense?
a Something suddenly happened.
b Something was going on for some time.

2 Complete the puzzle with the simple past of the verbs given.

across
1 sleep
3 blow
5 redo
7 drink
8 cut
11 speed
12 begin
13 think
15 hold
16 stand

down
1 strike
2 pay
3 bind
4 win
6 draw
9 teach
10 dream
11 seek
12 bite
14 have

3 Ask the questions in English.

Sie möchten wissen,
1 wo Bills Freund das Bild vom Altair zum ersten Mal sah.
2 wo Bill studierte.
3 ob es lange dauerte, das Programm zu entwickeln.
4 ob das Programm funktionierte, als sie es vorführten.
5 welchen Computer sie zur Entwicklung von BASIC benutzten.

1 _____
2 _____
3 _____
4 _____
5 _____

4 Ask questions about these sentences in the simple past.

1 Bill Gates helped to develop the MS-DOS system.
Who _____?

2 Bill's parents left him a lot of money.
What _____?

3 Computers already fascinated Bill in his early youth.
What _____?

4 Bill studied law at Harvard.
What _____?

5 One day Paul showed Bill a picture of the Altair computer.
What _____?

6 Bill and Paul developed BASIC.
Who _____?

5 Look at the sentences about one of Microsoft's newer products, Windows Vista, and fill in the simple past or the past continuous.

1 While developers at Microsoft _____ (work) on Windows Vista, they _____ (call) it by a code name – Longhorn.

2 A lot of people _____ (already wait) in the computer shop when Windows Vista _____ (be first sold).

3 Before Vista _____ (come out) many people _____ (debate) whether it would be as good as XP.

4 I _____ (look for) a new computer when Windows Vista _____ (be launched).

6 Make sentences using the simple past and the past perfect.

1 When / Microsoft / start to sell / Windows Vista / Windows XP / be on the market / for nearly six years
_____
_____

2 Bill Gates / be / the leading person in Microsoft / for 25 years/ when / he decide / to withdraw from the day to day business in the company
_____
_____

▶▶▶

19

3 Many computer manufacturers and business customers / try out / Windows Vista / before / Microsoft / release / the program worldwide

_____

_____

4 Many customers / who / use / Windows XP / be / very excited / when they / hear about / Vista

_____

_____

5 Microsoft / spend / an enormous amount of money on the development of Vista / but they / be pleased with / the result

_____

_____

_____

7 Complete with the simple past or the past perfect continuous.

1 Paul Allen and Bill Gates _____ (work) on the software for the Altair for 8 weeks before they _____ (sell) it to the company.

2 The reporter _____ (interview) Bill Gates for one hour when he _____ (get) a phone call from his editor.

3 Before Bill Gates and his wife Melinda _____ (form) a foundation [Stiftung] they _____ (donate) money to charity for many years.

4 A lot of people _____ (only use) Windows 95 for 5 years when they _____ (decide) to buy a new computer with Windows 2000.

5 When Bill Gates _____ (start) his own company he _____ (study) at Harvard for 3 years.

8 Put the words in the right order to make sentences.

1 After / left / had / Bill / Harvard / founded / he / Microsoft

_____

_____

2 What / had / been / Bill / doing / all the years / studied / before / he / at Harvard / ?

_____

_____

3 playing / I / a game / when / was / the computer / broke down

_____

_____

4 I / instead / I / so / where / had / my / remember / laptop / used / couldn't / the computer / put / I

_____

_____

5 never / switch off / before / forgotten to / my / computer / had / I

_____

_____

9 Computer problems: Circle the right form of the verb.

1 When I *tried to / was trying to / had tried to* access my files, it *took / was taking / had taken* ages for the files to open.

2 Yesterday my computer *was being / had been / were* on for about ten minutes when it suddenly *turned itself off / was turning itself off / had turned itself off*.

3 I *typed / had typed / had been typing* a letter on my computer for about a quarter of an hour when the letter suddenly *disappeared / was disappearing / had disappeared* from the screen.

4 After I *surfed / was surfing / had been surfing* the internet for a while, my computer *froze / was freezing / had frozen* [blockieren].

5   This morning I *put / was putting / had put* a jazz CD into my office computer. As I *didn't want / hadn't been wanting* anybody to hear it in the office I *was bringing / had brought / had been bringing* my headphones with me from home. Everybody in the office *worked / was working / had worked* when they *heard / were hearing / had heard* loud jazz music. I *was forgetting / had forgotten* to plug the headphones in. How embarrassing!

10 *Spot the problem and correct the wrong sentences. One sentence is already correct.*

1   I didn't hear about Windows Vista until I saw an article about it in the paper.

2   I didn't bought a new computer last year.

3   When I was young, I was wanting to be a computer expert.

4   I was typing an important letter when my computer stopped working.

5   I used Windows XP for two years when I bought a computer with Vista.

I did my homework but the computer ate it.

11 *A computer quiz. First circle the correct verb forms in the questions. Then put a ✓ next to the solution you know – or think – is correct.*

1   Bill Gates *studied / was studying* at Harvard when he developed his first programming language. But what did he study?
    a Mathematics [ ]
    b Law [ ]
    c Computer Science [ ]

2   The Microsoft Windows systems are very popular with computer users. When *did Microsoft release / was Microsoft releasing* the first one?
    a 1980 [ ]
    b 1985 [ ]
    c 1990 [ ]

3   How many Windows systems *had Microsoft launched / did Microsoft launch* previously when it started selling Windows Vista worldwide in 2007?
    a 7 [ ]
    b 15 [ ]
    c 22 [ ]

4   Bill Gates *worked / had been working* for Microsoft for 25 years when he resigned as CEO. When did he resign?
    a 1995 [ ]
    b 2000 [ ]
    c 2006 [ ]

5   There are more than 162 million websites online today. How many websites *were / had been* online in 1993?
    a 130 [ ]
    b 13,000 [ ]
    c 1.3 million [ ]

8 Past tenses B

Present perfect – present perfect continuous

A Present perfect vs. simple past

1 **Have** you **seen** the news report about Stromboli yet?
2 I'**ve been** interested in volcanoes for years.
3 The papers **have reported** a lot about the disaster.
4 I **watched** a TV programme about volcanoes last night.
5 Many tsunamis **hit** Asia between 1995 and 2004.

- Das **present perfect** wird für Vorgänge benutzt, die **in der Gegenwart noch andauern**. Der Zustand oder die Handlung hat zwar **in der Vergangenheit begonnen** (würde evtl. sogar beendet), schließt die Gegenwart jedoch mit ein. Signalwörter sind *already, always, at last, ever, finally, for* [seit], *in the meantime* [in der Zwischenzeit], *just* [gerade, eben], *lately/recently* [in letzter Zeit], *so far / to date / up to now* [bis jetzt], *since* [seit], *still (not) / (not) yet, this week/month/year* **(1, 2)**.
- Das *present perfect* wird benutzt, wenn der Zeitpunkt der Handlung nicht erwähnt wird, dafür aber ihre Folgen **(3)**.
- Das *simple past* dagegen wird für abgeschlossene Handlungen verwendet, die sich zu einem bestimmten Zeitpunkt **(4)** oder in einem bestimmten Zeitraum **(5)** in der Vergangenheit ereignet haben.

B Present perfect continuous

1 They'**ve been making** films about catastrophes for years.
2 Experts **have been trying** to develop a tsunami warning system since December 2004.
3 He says he'**s known** the solution the whole time.

- Das *present perfect continuous* **betont die Dauer** von Handlungen oder Zuständen, die in der Vergangenheit angefangen haben und zur Zeit des Sprechens noch nicht beendet sind **(1-2)**.
- Die *continuous-* und *simple*-Formen im *present perfect* sind häufig austauschbar aber einige Verben existieren in der Regel <u>nicht</u> in der *continuous*-Form: *be, believe, exist, know, like, see, understand, want* **(3)**.

Watch out!

1 „Seit" wird im Englischen entweder mit *since* (seit + Zeitpunkt) oder mit *for* (seit + Zeitraum) wiedergegeben: *I've been interested in volcanoes **for** many years / **since** 1995*.
2 „Gegenwart + schon" entspricht im Englischen die Verwendung des *present perfect continuous*, z.B. „Vulkane **verursachen** seit Jahrhunderten Probleme". = *Volcanoes **have been causing** problems for centuries now*.

Catastrophes

Active volcanoes can destroy cities or even cause tsunamis and earthquakes [*Erdbeben*]. Italy has three active volcanoes (which have erupted [*ausgebrochen*] in the last 100 years): Vesuvius, near Naples, Etna on Sicily and Stromboli on an island north-east of Sicily.

1 *Fill in the present perfect and circle any signal words.*

Breaking news – Stromboli erupts!

News _____ just _____ (come in)[1] that Stromboli _____ (erupt)[2] again after being inactive for several months. Luckily, the eruption _____ (not cause)[3] too much damage so far. But this may change as, according to the Italian media, the eruption produced a small tidal wave [*Flutwelle*], which _____ since _____ (reach)[4] the coast of Italy.

Despite early warning signs, the government _____ (be)[5] slow to react. However, new reports say that the Italian navy _____ finally _____ (start)[6] to evacuate island residents. These residents are anxious because, although Stromboli _____ (not be)[7] very active recently, experts _____ (describe)[8] this eruption as the start of a long period of new activity.

2 *Form sentences with the present perfect using the words below.*

1 the Stromboli volcano / become / well-known / in recent years

   _____
   _____

2 Etna / also attract / lots of attention over the decades

   _____
   _____

3 experts / always consider / Etna to be the more dangerous of the two volcanoes

   _____
   _____

4 they / still not decide / if Etna might erupt soon

   _____
   _____

5 there / not be / a major catastrophe / on Sicily yet

   _____
   _____

6 you / ever experience / an eruption first hand? – no, but I / see / the damage afterwards

   _____
   _____

3 *Present perfect or simple past? Complete this text about earthquakes in California. Circle any signal words.*

How long before the next huge quake?

In recent years there _____ (be)¹ many small earthquakes in California. But the worst one _____ (happen)² on April 18, 1906 and _____ (destroy)³ huge areas of San Francisco. The plates of the San Andreas Fault [San-Andreas-Graben] _____ (push)⁴ against each other and _____ (move)⁵ a total of 6 metres. April 18 was a Wednesday, a date San Franciscans _____ (still not forget)⁶, even though many of them were not alive then. On that Wednesday morning, fires _____ (break out)⁷ everywhere. In fact, most of the city _____ (burn)⁸ to the ground. About 3,000 people _____ (die)⁹ and approximately 300,000 _____ (lose)¹⁰ their homes. People _____ (be forced)¹¹ to live in tents provided by the army. Calculations _____ (recently show)¹² that the next big earthquake could happen soon. How bad will the damage be this time?

4 *Find twelve signal words in the puzzle. Which ones indicate the present perfect and which ones the simple past?*

K	L	A	S	T	J	O	N	B	E	Y
V	J	S	T	I	L	L	O	E	A	Z
E	I	A	I	L	B	R	A	D	N	M
V	C	L	B	N	W	N	R	F	A	O
E	A	A	R	E	C	E	N	T	L	Y
R	L	T	Q	K	T	E	D	O	W	U
H	E	E	U	S	W	H	E	N	A	G
Y	R	L	E	C	A	X	D	G	Y	F
M	I	Y	H	P	G	E	J	U	S	T
S	T	U	R	T	O	N	S	W	T	Y

Present perfect
since
_____
_____
_____
_____
_____
_____

Simple past
_____
_____
_____
_____
_____
_____
_____

23

5 Spot the problem and correct these sentences.

1 Etna didn't erupt recently.
_____

2 The San Andreas Fault moved several metres over 100 years.
_____

3 Several earthquakes occurred in California lately.
_____

4 Since about 1995 there are more hurricanes than usual in the Gulf of Mexico.
_____

5 The volcano didn't erupt yet.
_____

6 The German city of Freiburg has been hit by some small quakes last year.
_____

7 In the 1906 earthquake about 300,000 have been made homeless.
_____

8 The city didn't have any earthquakes up to now.
_____

6 Since or for? Circle the correct word in this text about life since the tsunami of 26 December 2004.

Since/For¹ the past year the countries hit by the tsunami have been trying hard to recover. Since/For² the moment it occurred – since/for³ December 2004 that is – life has never been the same. In western Indonesia, near the centre of the quake, half a million people have had to live without a proper home since/for⁴ nearly twelve months. And some of them have not eaten properly since/for⁵ weeks. But since/for⁶ yesterday, when more food and tents arrived, things will get better.

7 Finish the sentences with the correct ending – a or b.

1 Mount Etna hasn't erupted … .   **b**
   Mount Etna didn't erupt … .   **a**
   a last year
   b so far this year

2 A lot of people were killed … .   ☐
   A lot of people have been killed … .   ☐
   a in the 1906 earthquake
   b by earthquakes over the years

3 I became interested in volcanoes … .   ☐
   I have been interested in volcanoes … .   ☐
   a since watching the film, Volcano
   b after watching the film, Volcano

4 I started reading the book … .   ☐
   I have started reading the book … .   ☐
   a when I heard about it on TV
   b and am really enjoying it

5 There haven't been any earthquakes here for … .   ☐
   There haven't been any earthquakes here since … .   ☐
   a 1952   b a while

6 I have been researching tsunamis for … .   ☐
   I have been researching tsunamis since … .   ☐
   a years   b last year

8 Present perfect simple or continuous? Complete the text about buoys* [Boje] used to warn about tsunamis.

Sometimes there is more than one solution. Choose the best form in each case.

"… and so you see, ladies and gentlemen, we _____ (know)¹ for a while that a big tsunami could happen again at any time. We need a warning system, and we _____ just _____ (succeed)² in developing the right technology. Many countries _____ (live)³ with the danger of tsunamis for far too long already. Hundreds of thousands of people _____ (be killed)⁴ over the years. Over 600 people _____ (lose)⁵ their lives in the Pacific region this year alone. But for the past year and a half the USA _____ (work)⁶ on a tsunami buoy, which it _____ just _____ (lay)⁷ about 1,000 km from the west coast of Thailand. How long _____ the world _____ (dream)⁸ of something like this which could save thousands of lives?"
*pronounced 'boy'

9 *Rewrite these sentences using the present perfect (simple or continuous) and since or for.*

1. The last time the volcano erupted was in 1986.
   The volcano hasn't erupted since 1986.

2. Dr Smith started researching tsunamis years ago.
   _____
   _____

3. The volcano became active in 1645 and it is still active.
   _____
   _____

4. San Francisco's last major earthquake was in 1906.
   _____
   _____

5. I became interested in earthquakes when I was a child.
   _____
   _____

6. The US started making tsunami buoys a few years ago and are still making them.
   _____
   _____

10a *Translate these sentences.*

1. Der Ätna ist seit Jahrhunderten sehr aktiv.
2. In letzter Zeit sind viele Menschen bei [in] Tsunamis gestorben.
3. Im Dezember 2004 sind ungefähr 200.000 ums Leben gekommen.
4. Der Vulkan ist noch nicht ausgebrochen.
5. Sie reden schon den ganzen Tag über die neue Boje.
6. Ein großes Erdbeben hat sich vor 12 Stunden ereignet.
7. Der Orkan bläst [blow] nun schon seit zwei Tagen.
8. Die Opfer [victim] des Tsunamis warten schon seit Wochen auf Hilfe.
9. Das Erdbeben vom Jahre 1906 in San Francisco hat morgens um 5 Uhr begonnen.

10b *And now translate these sentences into German.*

10. Stuart has been writing a book about volcanoes for two years now.
11. Since Stromboli erupted last month, there have been two tidal waves [Flutwellen].
12. Fewer people have died since the new warning system was developed.
13. People in San Francisco have been waiting for the next big earthquake for decades.

11 *A catastrophe quiz. First circle the correct verb forms in the questions. Then put a ✓ next to the solution you know – or think – is correct.*

1. Krakatoa *was* / *has been* extremely active in recent years. In 1883 it *caused* / *has caused* the loudest explosion in the world. How far away could people hear it?

   a 1,000 kilometres away [ ]
   b 3,000 kilometres away [ ]
   c 5,000 kilometres away [ ]

2. Vesuvius *erupted* / *has erupted* many times since then, but it is best known for its eruption in 79 AD. It *destroyed* / *has destroyed* the city of:

   a Pompeii. [ ]
   b Messina. [ ]
   c Rome. [ ]

3. Tambora (in Indonesia) *didn't erupt* / *hasn't erupted* since 1967. When it *exploded* / *has exploded* over 200 years ago, it caused:

   a the biggest tsunami of the 19th century. [ ]
   b the biggest earthquake of the 19th century. [ ]
   c the biggest famine [Hungersnot] of the 19th century. [ ]

4. Europe *experienced* / *has experienced* a number of earthquakes. The worst one *was* / *has been* in 1755. 100,000 people died and it completely destroyed:

   a London. [ ]
   b Lisbon. [ ]
   c Lyons. [ ]

5. In 2005 a hurricane *caused* / *has caused* a flood in New Orleans and over $80 billion in damage. What was its name?

   a Kyril [ ]
   b Katrina [ ]
   c Kate [ ]

9 The future

1 The euro **will become** a very strong currency [*Währung*].
2 Maybe the UK **will use** the euro soon as well.
3 Jim assumes the UK **won't join** the euro for a long time.
4 You want to know more about the EU? **I'll give** you a book about it.

🟠 Das **will future** wird verwendet:
für Vorhersagen über Ereignisse, die mit (praktischer) Sicherheit eintreten werden (1); häufig mit Adverbien wie *maybe*, *perhaps*, *probably* (2), ferner mit Verben und Ausdrücken wie *assume* [annehmen], *believe*, *expect*, *forecast*, *hope*, *imagine*, *suppose*, *think*, *be afraid*, *be sure*, *it's clear/obvious that …*, *there's no doubt that…*, um Erwartungen, Hoffnungen oder Vermutungen über die Zukunft zu äußern (3); zum Ausdruck einer spontanen Entscheidung oder eines Angebotes (4).

5 In the years ahead the UK **is going to invest** huge sums of money in Africa.
6 With more and more computers at the workplace, a lot of jobs **are going to disappear**.

🟠 Das **going to future** wird verwendet:
für feste Absichten und Pläne (5); für ein bevorstehendes Ereignis, das aufgrund bestimmter Anzeichen absehbar ist (6).

7 Production of the new plane **starts** on 1 April in Poland.
8 They**'re opening** a big Indian restaurant in Bratislava this month.
9 I can call you when the meeting **ends**.

🟠 Wenn man über fest terminierte Vorgänge spricht (Fahrplan oder ein festgelegtes Programm) benutzt man das **simple present** (7); das **present continuous** in Verbindung mit einer Zeitangabe der (nahen) Zukunft drückt bereits entschiedene Pläne und Verabredungen aus (8).
🟠 In einem Nebensatz, der durch *as soon as*, *before*, *if*, *until*, *when* eingeleitet wird, verwendet man immer das *simple present* und niemals *will* oder *going to* (9).

10 At midnight tomorrow the new member states **will be entering** the EU.

🟠 Das **future continuous** (*will + be + -ing form*) wird benutzt, um auszudrücken, dass etwas zu einer bestimmten Zeit in der Zukunft im Gang sein wird (10).

11 By next year two more states **will have become** EU members.

🟠 Das **future perfect** (*will + have + past participle*) betont, dass etwas zu einem bestimmten Zeitpunkt in der Zukunft abgeschlossen sein wird (11).

The EU: the economy, the trends, the people

1 Match the sentences to the reasons for using the will or going to future.

1	The new project will be a big success.	A	Erwartung
2	I expect we will build the new plane in India.	B	Hoffnung
3	We're going to open a new factory in the next ten years.	C	Vermutung
4	I assume they'll have to move production to Eastern Europe.	D	bevorstehendes Ereignis
5	With costs rising we're going to have to reduce the number of workers.	E	fester Plan
6	I hope I won't lose my job when the company outsources to Asia.	F	Vorhersage

2 Find ten words which are often used with the will future.

P	S	F	S	U	P	P	O	S	E
R	B	E	L	I	E	V	E	I	R
O	R	T	J	L	P	P	H	M	V
B	O	M	A	Y	B	E	O	A	T
A	S	S	U	M	E	R	P	G	H
B	W	H	D	C	B	H	E	I	I
L	A	W	B	R	T	A	T	N	N
Y	Y	S	T	O	N	P	U	E	K
F	O	R	E	C	A	S	T	T	J
A	Q	H	O	P	D	B	N	R	T

3
Will or going to? Complete the text describing an expert's opinion on the EU economy in 2030. The words in green will help you find the best solution.

Probably there _____ (be)¹ millions without a job and slums _____ (develop)² in all the big cities [Vermutung]. Many workers _____ (have to)³ take jobs that only offer a minimum wage [Mindestlohn] and national economies _____ (vanish)⁴ [Vorhersage]. Big firms _____ (move)⁵ a lot of production to China and India in the next 20 years [feste Absicht], and I'm fairly sure that _____ (reduce)⁶ their costs [Erwartung]. Several car firms _____ (not build)⁷ any new factories after 2015 in the EU, and they _____ (close)⁸ their last few factories no later than the year 2030 [feste Absicht]. EU car makers probably _____ (not manage)⁹ to compete against super cheap cars like the Nano from the Indian company Tata Motors [Vermutung]. Most union leaders [Gewerkschaftsführer] don't believe they _____ (be able to)¹⁰ stop the trend in the direction of Asia [Vermutung]. Some experts expect that young Europeans _____ (start)¹¹ searching for work in Singapore or Bangalore, India – the Silicon Valley of Asia – rather than here [Erwartung]. All the EU member states _____ (invest)¹² billions in factories outside the EU in countries like Ukraine or Moldova [Vorhersage] – perhaps that _____ (mean)¹³ cheaper products [Vermutung], but it _____ (not lead)¹⁴ to a higher standard of living here because it _____ (not give)¹⁵ jobs to EU workers [Vorhersage]. In fact, many people are afraid it _____ (cause)¹⁶ more poverty than before [Erwartung].

4
Make sentences using will or going to.

1 I / not think / the UK / ever introduce / the euro
_____
_____

2 the company / build / a new factory in India / next year
_____
_____

3 the EU / probably expand / to include some new members
_____
_____

4 more people / lose their jobs / with more companies outsourcing
_____
_____

5 it be clear that / more people move / within the EU in the future
_____
_____

6 experts think / the euro / become a strong currency
_____
_____

5
Simple present or present continuous? Complete the text about the future of a German aerospace firm.

Ladies and gentlemen, as you all know Bonnier _____ (build)¹ a new 20-seat passenger aircraft next year, the Bo311. The design phase _____ (start)² on 15 January, and once production _____ (get)³ underway, we hope to sell about twelve aircraft a month. But first I _____ (have)⁴ a meeting this Friday in Delhi at our Indian subsidiary [Tochterfirma], Delhi Air, and as soon as I have settled certain details with them we can start work. Unfortunately, Bonnier has financial problems because of high wages here in the EU and Delhi Air's workers can manufacture the Bo311 at a lower price than is possible for us. At Easter, Delhi-Air _____ (advertise)⁵ for 2,500 new employees and in the autumn we _____ (reduce)⁶ the number of jobs here in our central office at Mayerhofen to 725. I'm afraid that we _____ (not increase)⁷ helicopter production here in Germany this summer as we had hoped. So, all the parts for the new plane _____ (be made)⁸ in India from the end of next year onwards. I also have to tell you that all production _____ (end)⁹ at our factories in France and Portugal at the beginning of December. The fact is that if wages in the EU _____ (remain)¹⁰ so high, then we won't be able to build planes like this here any longer.

6 Here are some opinions about the future of the EU. Put a ring around the best possible future form.

1 Stuart (Ireland)

I think Jean and I *enjoy / will enjoy / are enjoying*[1] working in New Zealand. We're sick of all the rules and regulations in the EU, but I don't expect we *are having / will have / are going to have*[2] any problems with the way of life 'down under'.

2 Jean (Ireland)

I agree, but perhaps a completely different school system *is going to be / is / will be*[1] hard for our son Bill at first. But if he *will take / takes / is taking*[2] things as they come, I imagine he *isn't going to have / doesn't have / won't have*[3] any trouble getting along with the kids in New Zealand. They say it's a lot like Britain.

3 Ruta (Estonia)

Well, I *sell / am selling / will have sold*[1] my little apartment here in Tallinn in the spring and then I *will plan / plan / am going to plan*[2] to look for a job as a journalist in London or in Dublin no later than May next year. I'm pretty sure that most of my journalist friends here *are giving up / give up / will give up*[3] their jobs here as well – the salaries here in Estonia just aren't all that good!

4 Zygi (Poland)

In recent years lots of Polish people have gone to live in Britain. My girlfriend wants me to stay here and keeps saying things like, "But Zygi, why exactly *do you emigrate / are you going to emigrate / are you emigrating*[1] now?" and "What sort of work *do you do / are you doing / are you going to do*[2] in the UK?" Well, the answer is simple. You see, with so much mechanization in my steel factory, I assume my job *vanishes / will vanish / is going to vanish*[3]. And sooner rather than later! So I *am leaving / will leave / will have left*[4] Warsaw for the UK this month. My new job as a waiter *is starting / starts / will have started*[5] in Oxford on 1 June.

5 Jan (Czech Republic)

It's clear that Brussels *improves / will improve / is going to improve*[1] the lives of us all in the EU eventually. So although our salaries *will increase / increase / are increasing*[2] here at my firm, it's obvious that I *am doing / do / will do*[3] a lot better working for our French parent company [*Mutterkonzern*] in Paris than here in Prague. So I *am probably trying / will probably try / will probably be trying*[4] my luck in Paris.

7 Read this part of a speech about the high numbers of EU migrants to Britain from Eastern Europe, and fill in the future continuous or the future perfect.

"… and so you see that, because of the many new citizens from eastern EU states, the government has decided to establish a new language programme. In the next eighteen months or so we _____ (train)¹ a number of policemen in big cities to speak Polish and by 2020 these language courses _____ (take place)² in all major cities. By the end of the decade, communication between police and EU migrants from Eastern Europe _____ (improve)³ greatly – I'm certain about that. Policemen who take part in our Polish course _____ (learn)⁴ enough after six months to have a basic conversation and, by the end of the course, they _____ (become)⁵ more or less fluent [fließend]. All of this costs money, of course, and I'm afraid that we _____ (not put)⁶ all our plans into practice within the next five years for financial reasons. And that brings me to my next point …"

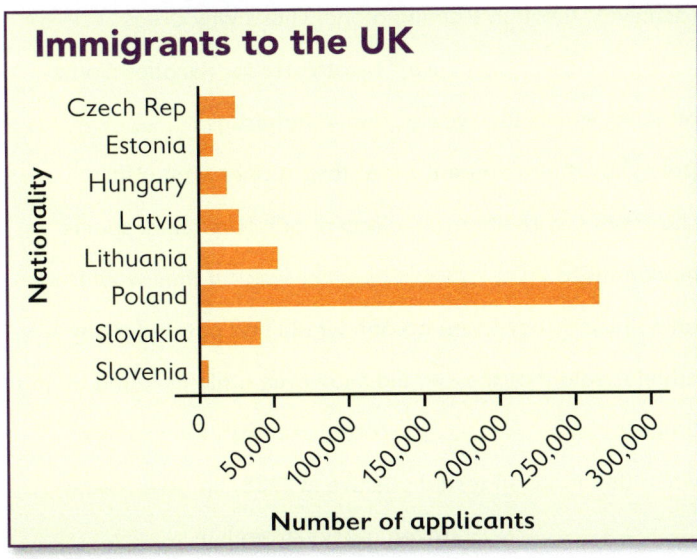

8 Translate the sentences using a future form.
Sometimes more than one solution is possible.

1 Es ist klar, dass ich die neue Stelle in Manchester nicht bekommen werde.
2 Wir hoffen, dass es einen Mindestlohn in der EU geben wird.
3 Sobald unser Land ein Mitglied der EU ist, werden unsere Löhne steigen.
4 Nächsten Monat werde ich in Madrid arbeiten.
5 Der Zug fährt heute Vormittag um 10.00 Uhr.
6 In diesem Frühjar eröffnen wir eine Tochterfirma in Tallinn.
7 Bis [*By*] Ende der Woche wird er seine Wohnung verkauft haben.
8 Zu Weihnachten beabsichtigt er, seinen Job aufzugeben.
9 Ich kann die Dokumente nicht finden. – Dann suche ich sie.
10 Bis wann wird die Türkei der EU beigetreten [*join*] sein?

9 Only one of these sentences is correct. Spot the problems and correct the wrong sentences.

1 I assume production doesn't start soon.
   _____
   _____

2 We probably don't finish the design work for another six months or so.
   _____
   _____

3 We are going to hire new workers when the contract has been signed.
   _____
   _____

4 We forecast that the market for small aircraft in India increases by 25%.
   _____
   _____

5 We need more time on the engine design before Delhi Air will decide on a final price.
   _____
   _____

6 As soon as I will have more information, I can email you again with the final details.
   _____
   _____

10 The passive

1. A lot of drugs …

are	sold	every year.
were	bought	last year.
have been	developed	recently.
will be	found	in the future.
can be	bought	illegally.

2. New drugs **are imported** every year.
3. Drugs have always been used **by athletes**.
4. **Some athletes were given** drugs without knowing it.
5. **It is said that** [Man sagt, dass] almost all cyclists took drugs in the past.

- Das Passiv wird aus den Formen von *be* + past participle gebildet **(1)**.
- Im Passiv wird oft die Person, von der etwas ausgeführt wird, nicht genannt, weil sie offensichtlich oder unwichtig ist **(2)**.
- Will man betonen, von wem etwas ausgeführt wurde, wird *by* + Person hinzugefügt **(3)**.
- Von einem Aktivsatz können Sie einen Passivsatz ableiten. Das direkte Objekt wird zum Subjekt des Passivsatzes.
  *They increase **the price of drugs** every year.*
  ***The price of drugs** is increased every year.*
- Auch das indirekte Objekt kann zum Subjekt eines Passivsatzes werden **(4)**.
  Ausdrücke, die vom Deutschen abweichen:
  I was shown = mir wurde gezeigt
  I was expected = von mir wurde erwartet
- Bei Verben wie *believe, consider, expect, know, report, say, think* kann man eine Passivkonstruktion mit *It is … that* bilden **(5)**.

Watch out!

1. Die Formen von *to be* im englischen Passiv werden meistens mit Formen von *werden* im deutschen Passiv übersetzt.
2. Sätze mit *man* sind oft Passivsätze im Englischen.

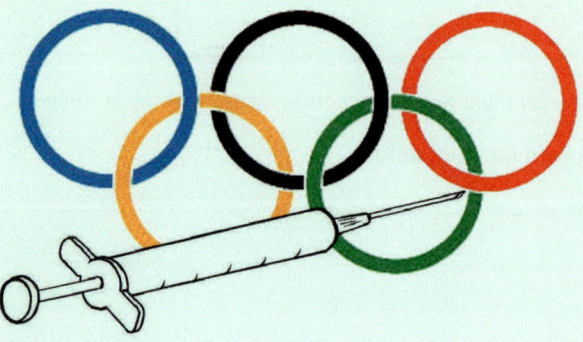

Doping in sports

1 *Underline all the passive verb forms in the text below.*

The term 'doping' is used to refer to drugs which improve sporting performance. Although it is often thought that doping has only recently become a problem, athletes have been using drugs for some time. At the end of the 19th century, for example, caffeine and cocaine were used by professional cyclists to reduce pain and tiredness. One famous incident happened during the Tour de France of 1967. After Tom Simpson, an English cyclist, collapsed, he was taken to a nearby hospital by helicopter where he died a short time later. Two tubes of drugs and one empty tube were later found in his racing jersey. This may have been an extreme case but the possible side effects of doping should not be ignored. It is thought that heart diseases and cancer could be caused by long-term doping but these suspicions have not been proven yet.

2 *Fill in the right passive forms of the verbs.*

Why do athletes use drugs?

Star athletes can earn a lot of money but the time in which they can do so _____ (limit)[1]. Some athletes think that top performance cannot _____ (achieve)[2] through training alone. That's why drugs _____ (use)[3] by athletes for decades. Some athletes, especially cyclists, know that drugs _____ (take)[4] by their competitors so they simply want a fair chance in competitions. In a recent poll [Umfrage], sports personalities _____ (ask)[5] if they would take drugs if they knew no one would find out and many athletes said that they would. However, athletes found taking drugs _____ (often punish)[6], for example when Ben Johnson tested positive in 1988, his gold medal _____ (taken away)[7] from him.

3 Make passive sentences. Then translate the passive sentences into German on a separate piece of paper.

1 Steroids / also use / to improve appearance
   Steroids are also used to improve appearance.
2 Steroids / use / by athletes / for years
   _____
3 Steroids / can detect / months after / they take
   _____
4 Steroids / cannot buy / legally
   _____
5 The use of steroids / ban / in all major sports
   _____
6 The side effects of steroids / still feel / in later life
   _____

4 Active or passive? Circle the right form.

1 Doctors *have reported* / *have been reported* serious side effects.
2 Two gold medals *took away* / *were taken away* by the Olympic Committee last year.
3 New drug tests *are developing* / *are being developed* at the moment.
4 All athletes *will test* / *will be tested* for drugs at the next competition.
5 The coach *gave* / *was given* her steroids for six months.
6 A lot of new cases of doping *have appeared* / *have been appeared* in the news recently.

5 Change these active sentences into passive sentences. Start the sentences with the underlined pronoun. Don't write who these things are done by.

1 The coach gave <u>him</u> an unknown drug.
   He was
2 Her parents did not allow <u>her</u> to use steroids.
   _____
3 The reporter asked <u>me</u> if I had ever taken any drugs.
   _____
4 The police found <u>some steroids</u> in the athlete's bag.
   _____
5 The sprinter bought <u>the drugs</u> illegally on the black market.
   _____

6 Translate the German expressions. Start the sentences with it and a passive verb form.

1 (*Man sagte*) that drugs don't help in all sports.
   It is
2 (*Man glaubt schon seit langer Zeit*) that drugs and crime are linked.
   _____
3 (*Man weiß*) that taking drugs is dangerous but this doesn't stop a lot of people.
   _____
4 (*Man hatte schon immer vermutet*) that drugs change the drug user's personality.
   _____

7 Write down four sentences that make a mini story. Start with words in the first row. Each word can only be used once.

Some drugs	The thief	We hope he	He
will be	were	may be	hasn't been
caught	sent	stolen	arrested
last week	soon	yet	to prison

1 _____
2 _____
3 _____
4 _____

8 Fill in the English passive verb forms.

1 It _____ (*ist herausgefunden worden*) that steroids can be addictive.
2 Drugs _____ (*werden gewöhnlich gekauft*) illegally on the black market.
3 The blood _____ (*wurde analysiert*) in a laboratory.
4 It _____ (*wird geglaubt*) that, in the future, drugs _____ (*werden benutzt werden*) which _____ (*können nicht entdeckt werden*).
5 The dangers of drugs _____ (*wurden ihm erklärt von*) a doctor.

Focus on ...
False friends and other problems

Als *false friends* bezeichnet man diejenigen Worte, die im Deutschen und Englischen gleich oder ähnlich geschrieben werden, jedoch nicht das Gleiche bedeuten (z.B. brav v. *brave* = tapfer).

Quiz A

Without using a dictionary, cross out any sentences where you think the English is wrong because of a false friend.

1. I got a really good note in the English test.
2. She left a note for you in the kitchen.
3. These are the worst notes I've ever had in maths.
4. These two notes are worth one hundred euros.

5. There are fifty teachers at our gymnasium.
6. You have to learn Latin at the gymnasium.
7. Rachel has judo classes in the gymnasium on Thursdays.

8. I want to be a photography when I'm older.
9. I want to be a photograph when I'm older.
10. I want to be a photo when I'm older.
11. I want to be a photographer when I'm older.

12. You can become a pizza at the restaurant over there.
13. You can get a pizza at the restaurant over there.

14. I'll become more if I get a better job.
15. She became ill after eating the pizza.

16. We spent the night in a Welsh pension.
17. Your pension depends on how much you earn.
18. Do you know any cheap pensions we can stay in on holiday?
19. All our employees get a pension.

20. He blames himself for the accident.
21. He's blamed himself again by being stupid.
22. He only has himself to blame for his problems.

23. When does the plane start?
24. When does the play start?

Look at the table below and then do exercises 1 and 2.

German meaning	English word	German false friend	English meaning
Handlung, Tat	action	Aktion	campaign
eigentlich; wirklich, tatsächlich	actual	aktuell	current, currently
(schmale) Gasse	alley	Allee	avenue
auch	also	also	so, therefore
werden	become	bekommen	get
jdm die Schuld geben	blame	sich blamieren	make a fool of oneself
tapfer, mutig	brave	brav	good, well-behaved
Küchenchef, Chefkoch	chef	Chef	boss
Christus	Christ	Christ	Christian
folglich, daher	consequently	konsequent	consistent
Turnhalle	gymnasium	Gymnasium	grammar school
Oberschule (USA)	high school (AE)	Hochschule	university, college
Arbeit(s-)	labour	Labor	lab(oratory)
Orangenmarmelade	marmalade	Marmelade	jam
Bedeutung	meaning	Meinung	opinion
Mord; ermorden	murder	Mörder	murderer
(Geld)Schein; Notiz; notieren	note	Note	mark (BE), grade (AE)
Altersrente, Pension	pension	Pension	guest house
Fotografie, Bild	photograph	Fotograf	photographer
vernünftig	sensible	sensibel	sensitive
anfangen	start	starten	to take off
mitfühlend	sympathetic	sympathisch	likeable

1 *Translate the missing parts of the sentences.*

1 Was ist *deine Meinung* über die königliche Familie?

   What's _____ of the royal family?

2 *Diese Bedeutung* des Wortes ist ungewöhnlich.

   _____ of the word is unusual.

3 *Unser Gymnasium* besitzt eine sehr moderne *Turnhalle*.

   _____ has a very modern _____ .

4 Das ist gewiss *eine vernünftige Idee*.

   That's certainly _____ .

5 *Eigentlich* glaube ich, dass AIDS das schlimmste von allen *aktuellen* Problemen ist.

   _____ I think that AIDS is the worst of all _____ problems.

6 *Die tatsächliche Gefahr* war sehr gering.

   _____ was very small.

7 Er *wird* eine Stelle an einer *Hochschule bekommen*.

   He'll _____ a place at a _____ .

8 Sie unterrichtet an *einer Oberschule* in den USA.

   She teaches at _____ in the USA.

9 Ben ist *ein braver, sehr sensibler Junge*.

   Ben is _____ .

10 Es wäre interessant, *in einem Labor zu arbeiten*.

   It would be interesting _____ .

11 Ute kaufte *eine kleine Pension* mit einem Teil von *ihrer Altersrente*.

   Ute bought _____ with part of _____ .

12 *Tapfer* ist er ja, aber nicht gerade *sympathisch*.

   He's _____ all right, but he's not exactly _____ .

13 Sei *konsequent* in dem, was du machst.

   Be _____ in what you do.

14 Paris ist eine Mischung aus *alten Gassen und eleganten Alleen*.

   Paris is a mixture of _____ .

2 Mark each sentence as right [✓] or wrong [✗] and then correct any wrong sentences. Three sentences are already correct.

1 [ ] Every Christian believes in Christus.

2 [ ] The current advertising action will be expensive.

3 [ ] Who's the chef of this company?

4 [ ] She acted consequently – that's why she's been successful.

5 [ ] The labor market in the USA is in a difficult situation.

6 [ ] We design PCs in our labor.

7 [ ] After my father died, everyone was very sympathetic towards me.

8 [ ] He can cook better than any of the chefs at the Ritz hotel.

Quiz B

Without using a dictionary, cross out any sentences where the English is wrong with regard to singular or plural forms.

1 His knowledges of English must be good.
2 His knowledge of English must be good.
3 His English knowledges must be good.

4 She earned one thousand dollar in two month.
5 She earned one thousand dollars in two month.
6 She earned one thousand dollar in two months.
7 She earned one thousand dollars in two months.

8 No progress has been made.
9 No progresses have been made.
10 No progress have been made.

11 The good news has surprised me.
12 A good news has surprised me.
13 The good news have surprised me.

14 Nowadays the most people don't go to church.
15 Nowadays most of the people don't go to church.
16 Nowadays most people don't go to church.
17 Nowadays the most of the people don't go to church.

18 We gave her a good advice.
19 We gave her good advice.
20 We gave her good advices.

Viele Fehler deutschsprachiger Sprecher des Englischen resultieren daraus, dass die Besonderheiten des Englischen nicht berücksichtigt werden. Ein Beispiel: Ein deutscher Plural entspricht gelegentlich einem englischen Singular, z.B. Schäden = *damage*.
(Das Wort *damages* dagegen bedeutet Schadenersatz.)

Look at the table below and then do exercise 3.

A Substantiv und Verb im Singular	Beispiel: Your advice was useful.
advice	Ratschläge (*a piece/word/bit of advice* = ein Ratschlag)
damage	Schäden
furniture	Möbel (*a piece of furniture* = ein Möbelstück)
hair	Haare
information	Informationen (*a piece of / some information* = eine Information)
knowledge	Kenntnisse (*knowledge of ...* = (Englisch)Kenntnisse)
news	Nachrichten (*a piece / bit of / some news* = eine Nachricht)
progress	Fortschritte
B Substantiv und Verb im Plural	**Beispiel: Your sunglasses are in the drawer.**
binoculars	Fernglas
contents	Inhalt
glasses	Brille
goods	(Handels-)Ware
outskirts	Außen-, Randgebiet
scissors	Schere
surroundings	Umgebung
trousers	Hose
C Substantiv Plural, Verb Singular	**Beispiel: Darts is a popular pastime.**
darts	Darts
the Netherlands	die Niederlande
politics	Politik
the United Nations (UN)	die Vereinigten Nationen
the United States (USA)	die Vereinigten Staaten

Watch out!

1 Das Englische unterscheidet sich in vielem vom Deutschen, wie z.B. *die meisten Leute* = *most people*; *zwanzig Dollar* = *twenty dollars*; *fünf Euro* = *five euros*; *zwei Monate* = *two months* (Das *s* bei *month* wird häufig vergessen, da die Deutschen dies nur schwer aussprechen können).

2 Das Wort *police* wird immer als Plural behandelt z.B. *the police **are** here*.

3 *Translate the missing word(s) and then circle the correct verb form.*

1 Viele *Schäden* sind gemacht worden.

A lot of _____ *has / have* been done.

2 *Mein Fernglas* liegt auf dem Rucksack.

_____ *is lying / are lying* on the rucksack.

3 *Seine Französischkenntnisse* waren ausgezeichnet.

_____ *was / were* excellent.

4 *Ein guter Ratschlag* hilft im richtigen Moment.

_____ *help / helps* at the right moment.

5 *Deine guten Ratschläge* waren sehr nützlich.

_____ *was / were* very useful.

6 Guten Abend! Sie hören die *Nachrichten*.

Good evening! Here *is / are* the _____ .

7 *Keine Nachrichten* sind *gute Nachrichten*.

_____ *is / are* _____ .

8 *Die Vereinigten Staaten* besitzen viele Waffen.

_____ *possess / possesses* a lot of weapons.

9 *Die meisten Leute* genießen einen Strandurlaub.

_____ *enjoy / enjoys* a holiday on the beach.

10 *Die Ware* wiegt zweihundert *Kilo*.

_____ *weighs / weigh* 200 _____ .

11 *Politik* ist ein hartes Geschäft.

_____ *is / are* a hard business.

12 *Einige neue Informationen* sind gerade eingetroffen.

_____ *has / have* just arrived.

I need a new glass.

Test 2

Present tenses (▶ S. 16)

1 *Free time*
Translate these sentences using the simple present and the present continuous.

1 Ich gehe gerne in die Disko am Wochenende.
_____

2 – Was machst du gerade? – Ich lese ein Buch.
_____

3 Heute ist Samstag und ich spiele Fußball. Normalerweise spiele ich aber nur freitags.
_____

Past tenses A (▶ S. 18)

2 *J. K. Rowling and Harry Potter*
Finish the sentences using the simple past, the past continuous or the past perfect.

1 Rowling first _____ (get) the idea for Harry Potter while she _____ (sit) in a train from London to Manchester.

2 Rowling _____ (not start) writing her first Potter book when she _____ (give) birth to her daughter at the age of 26.

3 At the beginning of her career, Rowling sometimes _____ (work) on her book in a cafe while her little daughter _____ (sit) next to her. She _____ (not have) enough money to pay for a babysitter and the cafe _____ (be) warmer than her flat.

4 When Harry Potter _____ (appear) on the New York Times bestseller list in 1999, Rowling _____ (already publish) three Harry Potter books.

5 The seventh copy of 'The Tales of Beedle the Bead' _____ (raise) 1.95 million pounds at auction. Rowling was glad that nobody _____ (film) her reaction when the book was finally sold. She was delighted that Amazon _____ (buy) the book to give money to a children's charity.

Past tenses B (▶ S. 22)

3 *Unemployment*
Simple past, present perfect or present perfect continous? Fill in the **best possible** solution in each case.

A Why _____ the government _____¹ (not do) more to help young people who are unemployed?

B I think we _____² (try) really hard to give young people work with different programmes last year. And the government _____³ (cooperate) with local councils more than ever. I feel things _____⁴ (improve) in recent months.

A The opposition says that you _____⁵ (not invest) enough money in new jobs in the budget.

B Well, we _____⁶ (hope) for some time for an improvement in the economy. We use money from taxes so I'm afraid we _____⁷ (not have) enough to properly finance these programmes recently.

The future (▶ S. 26)

4 *Holidays*
Circle the best possible future form.

1 This time next year I *will be swimming / am going to swim / am swimming* in the sea.
2 I don't think the weather *is going to be / will be / is* better when we're on holiday.
3 The next train *is going to leave / leaves / will leave* at 6 p.m.
4 I promise I *won't buy / am not going to / am not buying* so many souvenirs again.
5 I have planned a lot of holidays. By December I *will have been / will be / am going to be* to Peking, New York and Bali.

The passive (▶ S. 30)

5 *Computers*
Write sentences using the passive. Be careful with the tenses.

1 20 years ago / computers / mostly / use / in offices
_____

2 Today / more home computers / buy / than office ones
_____

3 Work / greatly / change / by computers
_____

11 Reported speech

1 *An immigrant:* I **want** to improve my English. [**simple present**]
The immigrant **pointed out** (that) he **wanted** to improve his English. [**simple past**]
2 *A politician:* More and more immigrants **are moving** here. [**present continuous**]
The politician **explained** (that) more and more immigrants **were moving** here. [**past continuous**]
3 *A British citizen:* I'**ve met** a lot of nice immigrants. [**present perfect**]
A British citizen **mentioned** (that) he **had met** a lot of nice immigrants. [**past perfect**]
4 *An immigrant:* I **didn't speak** English in the beginning. [**simple past**]
The immigrant **said** (that) he **hadn't spoken** English in the beginning. [**past perfect**]
5 *A worried citizen:* **Will** new immigrants **adjust** to British culture? [**will**]
A worried citizen **asked whether/if** new immigrants **would adjust** to British culture. [**would**]
6 *An immigration advisor:* Mustafa, **learn** English and **don't break** any laws.
The immigration advisor **told/advised** me **to learn** English and **not to break** any laws.
7 *Shop owner:* **Are** you **interested** in working in my shop?
The shop owner **asked** me **if/whether** I **was interested** in working in his shop.

- Steht in der indirekten Rede das einleitende Verb in der Vergangenheit, werden in der indirekten Rede andere Zeiten als in der direkten Rede verwendet (1–7).
- Enthalten Fragen in der direkten Rede kein Fragewort, steht *if* oder *whether* in der indirekten Rede (5, 7).
- Nach dem die indirekte Rede einleitenden Verb *tell* stehen Namen oder Pronomen (6).
- Befehle werden mit *tell* + *object* + *infinitive* (6), Ratschläge mit *advise* + *object* + *infinitive* (6) und Bitten mit *ask* + *object* + *infinitive* wiedergegeben (5,7).
- Wie im Deutschen muss man immer bedenken, dass aus der Sicht des Berichtenden Ort, Zeit und Personen anders als in der direkten Rede ausgedrückt werden müssen.

today	that day
yesterday	the day before
two days ago	two days before
last week	the week before / the previous week
tomorrow	the next/following day
next week	a week later / the following week

Watch out!

Nach *tell* nennt man die Person, der etwas gesagt wurde. Wird die Person nicht genannt, verwendet man *say* z.B. *He told me that …*
ABER *He said that …*

Multicultural society in the UK

1 *Read the speech bubbles and complete the text below.*

> Cultural differences are what has made Britain great. The UK has been a multicultural country for hundreds of years. Why is it such a big deal now? I think it is wonderful to live with different cultures and races and to learn from one another. For me a multicultural society is one where people can learn to live together peacefully and to respect each others' ways of life.

Jennifer Baird, London

> I'm a postman. You can't find a greater mixture of cultures anywhere. Sadly I have to admit that not everyone feels how I do. I only see nice people and nasty people regardless of colour, race or religion. We have always had a mixed culture and the sooner we accept this the stronger the country will be.

Arthur Peters, York

While talking to people about multicultural societies I heard some interesting opinions. Jennifer Baird from London praised the variety of cultures that _____ [1] Britain great. She pointed out that the UK _____ [2] a multicultural country for hundreds of years. She wondered why it _____ [3] such a big deal now. She thought it _____ [4] wonderful to live with different cultures and races and to learn from each other. For her a multicultural society was one where people _____ [5] to live together peacefully and respect each others' ways of life. Arthur Peters from York said that you _____ [6] a greater mixture of cultures than in his job as a postman. He regretted to say that he _____ [7] to admit that not everyone _____ [8] how he did. He explained he only _____ [9] nice people and nasty people regardless of colour, race or religion. He added that we _____ [10] a mixed culture and the sooner we _____ [11] this the stronger the country would be.

2 *Write down these questions from a radio phone-in programme in reported speech.*

- What has the government done to help immigrants with integration?
- What are the advantages of having immigrants?
- Will the economy get weaker with so many immigrants?
- Should immigrants learn the English language?
- Will immigrants lose their cultural identity if they adjust to 'British' culture?
- Why don't British people try to make it easier for foreigners to integrate?

The callers wanted to know

1 _____
2 _____
3 _____
4 _____
5 _____
6 _____

3 *A new immigrant has been given some advice. Complete his email below using the information in the box.*

> You must improve your English.
> Don't only talk to people from your country.
> You must try to understand British culture and learn about British history.
> Don't break any laws.
> Try to find work in a British company.

New email

Hi John

As you know I've just moved to Birmingham. The lady I live with has given me some advice about integrating. She told me that I _____ ¹ my English and _____ ² to people from my country. She _____ ³ British culture and learn about British history. She also _____ ⁴ any laws and _____ ⁵ work in a British company. She was quite helpful actually. Have you got any more advice for me?

Achmed

4 *Complete the text below with the missing parts of reported speech.*

Achmed Hi John. I've got a job interview today.
John Really? I thought you were working in the restaurant on Perkins Lane.
Achmed I was but I lost my job last week.
John That's a shame. Let me know if it goes well.
Achmed Of course. I will call you tomorrow if I get the job.

I met Achmed last week and he told me he _____ ¹ a job interview _____ ². He said that he _____ ³ old job _____ ⁴. He said he _____ ⁵ me _____ ⁶.

5 *Spot the problem and correct the wrong sentences. Two sentences are already correct.*

1 "I've lost my job."
   ▶ Achmed told that he had lost his job.
   _____
   _____

2 "I want to move to Britain."
   ▶ Zara says she wanted to move to Britain.
   _____
   _____

3 "I think multiculturalism is a positive development."
   ▶ She said that multiculturalism was a positive development.
   _____
   _____

4 "I read a report about immigration in my local paper last week."
   ▶ He said he had read a report in my local paper last week.
   _____
   _____

5 "Today's young people are used to a multicultural society."
   ▶ She remarked that today's young people were used to a multicultural society.
   _____
   _____

37

12 Modal auxiliaries A

can – be able to – be allowed to – may

1. Modern medicine **can** help people to live longer.
2. In 1996 scientists **could** / **were able** to clone a sheep. Its name was Dolly.
3. Some people think that scientists **will be able to clone** human beings soon.
4. Fortunately they **have not been able** to clone people yet.
5. **Were** you **able to** / **Could** you find that book about cloning yesterday? Yes, luckily I **was able to** buy it at the book shop.
6. Scientists
   can't / **may not** / **aren't allowed to**
   couldn't / **weren't allowed to**
   won't be allowed to
   haven't been allowed to
   clone people.
7. **Can/May** I ask you some questions about cloning?

- Man benutzt *can*, um über eine Fähigkeit zu sprechen (1). Die Ersatzform *be able to* (2-4) wird in der Gegenwart kaum benutzt; in der Vergangenheit ist sie weitgehend austauschbar mit *could* (2). In der Zukunft (3) und im *present perfect* (4) muss eine Form von *be able to* verwendet werden, da es keine Form von *can* gibt.
- Wenn man sagen will, was man in einer Einzelsituation geschafft hat, benutzt man *was/were able to*. In Fragen und verneinten Sätzen kann man auch *could* verwenden (5).
- *Can, may, be allowed to* benutzt man, um Erlaubnis auszudrücken. Bei Aussagen in der Gegenwart können alle drei Formen austauschbar benutzt werden. Bei Aussagen in der Vergangenheit können *couldn't* oder *wasn't allowed to* benutzt werden, für alle anderen Zeitformen von „dürfen" muss die Ersatzform *be allowed to* benutzt werden (6).
- Bei Fragen um Erlaubnis benutzt man *can* oder *may* (7), wobei *may* etwas höflicher klingt.

Watch out!
Can/Could kann im Sinne von **dürfen** (*permission*) und **können** (*ability*) benutzt werden.

The times are changing

1 *Circle the right modal form. Then put the letters into the boxes below to get a word used in this exercise.*

organ

1	2	3	4	5	6	7	8	9	10	11
r										

Today scientists [r] *can* / [a] *will be able to* [1] create stem cells [Stammzellen] from adult cells by inserting a few genes. Soon we [n] *can't* / [e] *will be able to* [2] duplicate human organs which can be used as human organ replacements.

20 years ago computer companies [t] *have not been able to* / [p] *couldn't* [3] imagine that most households today [l] *would be able to* / [r] *were able to* [4] afford a computer.

In 1966, Arthur C. Clarke wrote in Vogue magazine that houses [f] *will be able to* / [a] *would be able to* [5] fly by 2001.

Although robots [c] *have been able to* / [m] *are able to* [6] make cars and other products for some years, it will take quite some time until they [e] *are able to* / [r] *could* [7] work and think independently.

With medicine becoming more and more powerful we [a] *can't* / [m] *will be able to* [8] prevent aging as effectively as we [e] *can* / [g] *have been able to* [9] cure diseases today.

We [u] *can* / [n] *have been able to* [10] explore the solar system for many years with unmanned spacecraft. In some years we [t] *will be able to* / [d] *were able to* [11] send humans to Mars.

2 *Complete the sentences with the right form of can, be able to or be allowed to.*
Sometimes there are two possibilities.

1 In Germany scientists _____ create stem cells from human embryos. But maybe they _____ do so soon.

2 Should doctors _____ help patients to die? Most laws say no. However, doctors _____ stop life prolonging [*lebens verlängernd*] medical treatment if the patient wants it.

3 People who oppose the death penalty [*Todesstrafe*] say that the state _____ to kill people for far too long. However, some people who support the death penalty think that if we _____ deter [*abschrecken*] criminals from committing crimes, we will be able to stop crime altogether.

4 People _____ normally go shopping in Germany on Sunday now but they _____ go shopping on Sunday in the future.

5 We _____ travel to Mars yet but we _____ do so in the future.

6 People _____ smoke on the street now but they might _____ smoke there in the future.

7 Should people _____ to buy guns for private use?

3 *Use the modal verbs be able to, be allowed to or may to rewrite these sentences.*

1 Doctors can't clone people legally.
   Doctors aren't allowed to clone people.

2 Can I ask you some questions about your religion?
   _____

3 Robots can't think yet.
   _____

4 You can't smoke in German restaurants.
   _____

5 I couldn't understand what he said.
   _____

4 *Spot the problem and correct these sentences. Two sentences are already correct.*

1 In the future cars can fly.
   _____

2 When the scientists created the robot, he has been able to make simple decisions.
   _____

3 The doctor couldn't to cure his patient.
   _____

4 The computer was very powerful but it may not answer the question.
   _____

5 In 1969 the spacecraft Apollo 11 could travel to the moon.
   _____

6 Many authors have written stories about what we are able to do in the future.
   _____

7 Scientists have been able to find cures for many diseases.
   _____

8 Could we find life on Mars in the future?
   _____

5 *Translate these sentences.*

1 Früher durften Kinder den Eltern nicht widersprechen.
2 Durftest du zu Hause rauchen?
3 Werden wir die globale Erwärmung stoppen können?
4 Roboter konnten schon seit einigen Jahren Autoteile zusammensetzen.
5 Es sollte nicht erlaubt sein, Embryos zur Herstellung von Stammzellen zu benutzen.
6 Darf ich dir ein paar Fragen zur Stammzellforschung stellen? (*höfliche Frage*)
7 Sollten Wissenschaftler Menschen klonen dürfen?

13 Modal auxiliaries B

must – have to – needn't – used to – should – ought

1 Don't forget, you **must** have a visa if you travel to China.
2 The guide says that we **have to** be back by 12 o'clock.
3 How much **did** you **have to** pay for your visa?
4 You **don't have to** / **needn't** get a new credit card – yours is still valid.
5 You **mustn't** smoke in German restaurants.
6 A lot of things in China are so strange that you **may not** / **might not** believe them.
7 I **used to** take a lot of cash with me when I went on holiday. Now I use a credit card.
8 You **shouldn't** write down your pin number, you **ought to** memorize it.

- *Must* entspricht dem deutschen „müssen" und existiert nur in der Gegenwart **(1)**. Für alle anderen Zeiten verwendet man eine Form von *have to* **(2, 3)**. *Must* und *have to* sind weitgehend austauschbar.
- Mit *must* drückt der Sprecher aus, dass er etwas für zwingend erforderlich hält.
- *Have to* entspricht auch dem deutschen „müssen" und wird bevorzugt, wenn der Sprecher eine Anweisung weitergeben will **(2)**. Fragen werden fast immer mit *have to* gebildet **(3)**.
- *Needn't* und *don't have to* im Sinne von „nicht brauchen" sind gleichbedeutend **(4)**.
- *Mustn't* wird oft fälschlicherweise mit einer Form von „nicht müssen" übersetzt. Es muss jedoch mit einer Form von „nicht dürfen" übersetzt werden **(5)**.
- *May* und *might* drücken Unsicherheit aus. Es gibt keinen wesentlichen Unterschied zwischen den beiden Formen **(6)**.
- *Used to* drückt gewohnheitsmäßige Handlungen in der Vergangenheit aus **(7)**.
- *Should* und *ought to* dienen dem Ausdruck von Aufforderungen und Ratschlägen; sie sind weitgehend austauschbar **(8)**.

Watch out!

mustn't = nicht dürfen; *needn't* = nicht müssen

Travelling abroad – some useful tips

1 *Look at these tips about money and circle the right word – must, mustn't or needn't.*

When you travel abroad you *must / mustn't / needn't*[1] take enough money or a credit card with you to cover your expenses but you *must / mustn't / needn't*[2] change money in your home country. When you change money at home you *must / mustn't / needn't*[3] often pay more than in your country of destination. You *must / mustn't / needn't*[4] change money on the street – you could be given forged [*gefälscht*] notes.

It is very convenient to have a credit card so you *must / mustn't / needn't*[5] carry a lot of cash in a money belt. If you want to get money from the ATM you *must / mustn't / needn't*[6] have a pin number. It is a good idea to memorize your pin number so you *must / mustn't / needn't*[7] worry if the card gets stolen.

2 *Make sentences with might.*

1 Perhaps travelling to Canada is cheaper than travelling to America.

Travelling to Canada _____
_____ .

2 Perhaps the weather in Spain will be worse than it is here.

The weather in Spain _____
_____ .

3 It is possible that the guide has given us the wrong information.

The guide _____
_____ .

4 Perhaps we will have to wait a long time for the next train.

We _____
_____ .

3 Fill in the right form of have to. You sometimes have to use negative forms.

Interviewer   How much _____ you _____ ¹ pay for your flight to Germany?

Tourist   I _____ ² pay about 1200 dollars for the return flight which was more than I had originally wanted to pay. But I _____ ³ fly on one particular day so I couldn't get a cheaper ticket.

Interviewer   _____ ⁴ open your suitcase at the German customs control?

Tourist   No, I _____ ⁵. Actually I _____ never _____ ⁶ open my suitcase on any of my trips so far.

Interviewer   Did the Germans understand you?

Tourist   Oh yes, most of them did. You know, all Germans _____ ⁷ learn English at school but I still _____ ⁸ use my English–German dictionary sometimes. The fact that everybody can speak reasonable English is very convenient for Americans because they _____ ⁹ learn a foreign language. But to really be able to understand foreign people and their culture Americans _____ ¹⁰ learn more foreign languages in the future.

4 Complete this advice with mustn't, needn't or should. Sometimes there may be more than one possibility.

Travellers:

_____ ¹ take warnings of terrorist attacks seriously.

_____ ² necessarily have travel insurance but it is good to have it.

_____ ³ have a valid passport.

_____ ⁴ take weapons or knives onto the plane.

_____ ⁵ learn about the culture and history of the country they are going to.

_____ ⁶ take a credit card with them and only a little cash.

_____ ⁷ respect the laws of foreign countries, as they may be different from at home.

_____ ⁸ book their flight in a travel agency, they can also book online.

5 Circle the correct words.

1 Today people often book holidays on the internet, in the past they *used to / didn't use to* book them at travel agencies.

2 Today travellers are afraid of terrorists, they *used to / didn't use to* be afraid before 9/11.

3 Today they often go on short trips but they *used to / didn't use to* go on longer journeys when they were younger.

4 Today they expect price reductions, in the past they *used to / didn't use to* expect budget holidays.

5 Today last minute bookings are popular, in the past people *used to / didn't use to* make travel arrangements long before departure.

6 Underline the right modal verb to complete the missing word below.

1 [l] Do you have to
  [a] Mustn't you   have a visa for China?
  [c] May you

2 Tourists   [i] aren't allowed to
           [b] don't have to   take knives on a plane.
           [g] needn't

3 The passengers   [c] ought to
                 [u] mustn't   do what the pilot says.
                 [k] are allowed to

4 You   [o] needn't
      [e] mustn't   smoke during a flight.
      [p] shouldn't

5 I   [n] used to
    [r] ought to   travel with a backpack when I was young.
    [t] should

6 [c] Will he be able to
  [h] Will he be allowed to   learn English so quickly?

7 Marion   [d] shouldn't have
         [e] didn't use to   eat fast food in America.

In some foreign countries you need an international driving

1	2	3	4	5	6	7
l						

7 Translate these sentences.

1 In manchen Staaten müssen ausländische Autofahrer einen internationalen Führerschein haben.
2 Du darfst in deutschen Restaurants rauchen.
3 In der Vergangenheit mussten Deutsche ein Visum für die Vereinigten Staaten haben.
4 Für internationale Flüge brauchst du nicht länger als zwei Stunden vor dem Abflug am Flughafen sein.
5 Warum musstest du am Sonntag fliegen?

14 If-clauses

- Es gibt im Prinzip drei unterschiedliche Arten von *if*-Sätzen. Wichtig ist die Zeitenfolge des *if*-Satzes [*if-clause*] und des Hauptsatzes [*main clause*].

A Typ 1

1. **If** we **don't halt** climate change, we'll regret it.
2. We **can help** the planet **if** we **stop** using oil.
3. **If** you **travel** around Europe, **take** the train.
4. **If** cars **consume** petrol, they **produce** CO_2.

- Im *if*-Satz vom Typ 1 steht das *simple present*. Man benutzt im Hauptsatz *will* **(1)**, ein Hilfsverb wie *can* **(2)** oder einen Imperativ **(3)**.
- Bei allgemeingültigen Aussagen kann man das *simple present* in **beiden** Teilen des *if*-Satzes verwenden **(4)**.
- *If*-Sätze vom Typ 1 drücken eine wahrscheinliche Bedingung aus.

B Typ 2

If the air **became** better, my health **would improve**.

- Im *if*-Satz vom Typ 2 steht das *simple past*. Im Hauptsatz steht *would, could, might* mit Infinitiv.
- *If*-Sätze vom Typ 2 drücken eine Bedingung aus, die theoretisch möglich, aber kaum wahrscheinlich ist. Obwohl die Vergangenheitsform im *if*-Satz steht, bezieht die Bedingung sich auf die Gegenwart/Zukunft.

C Typ 3

If we **had used** fewer fossil fuels, we **would have created** fewer greenhouse gases.

- Im *if*-Satz steht das *past perfect* und im Hauptsatz *would, could* oder *might* + *have* + Partizip.
- *If*-Sätze vom Typ 3 drücken eine nicht mehr erfüllbare Bedingung aus. Die Bedingung bezieht sich auf die Vergangenheit.

Watch out!

1. Sowohl *would* wie auch *will* werden in aller Regel **nicht** im *if*-Teil des Satzes verwendet.
2. Steht der *if*-Teil des Satzes am Satzanfang, wird er durch ein Komma abgetrennt:
   If we don't do something, we'll regret it. / We'll regret it if we don't halt climate change.
3. Man bevorzugt in einem *if*-Satz *were* anstelle von *was*: *If I were you, I'd try to save energy.*

Climate change

China will build another 562 coal plants like this in the next ten years!

1 Here are some facts about climate change and its effects. Fill in the if-clauses type 1.

1. If China _____ (decide) to build 562 more coal plants [*Kohlekraftwerke*] in the coming years, it _____ (not make) life better for any of us in the future.
2. If CO_2 emissions _____ (increase) further, temperatures _____ (rise).
3. If the snow in the Alps _____ (melt), it _____ (cause) floods in the valleys below.
4. Many Germans _____ (prefer) to spend their summer holidays at the Baltic if the average summer temperature there _____ (rise).
5. If the ice in Greenland _____ (start) to melt, Denmark _____ (be able) to look for oil there.
6. The planet _____ (be) 2°C hotter in 2030 if CO_2 levels _____ (stay) high.

2 Some simple truths: what are we doing wrong? Fill in the simple present in the if-clause and the main clause.

If in twenty years time we _____ (be able to)[1] sunbathe on the beach in Alaska, something _____ (have to)[2] be wrong. But if we _____ (start)[3] doing something for the environment now, we _____ (can)[4] maybe alter how extreme climate change will be. And there are some small things that everyone can do to help. For example, if you _____ (travel)[5] short distances by car, you _____ (cause)[6] unnecessary pollution. It's only a small change, but if you _____ (take)[7] the bus or _____ (walk)[8] instead, you _____ (help)[9] to reduce pollution levels. It's the same with flying. If discount flights _____ (be)[10] cheap, more and more people _____ (fly)[11] to their destinations, even if they _____ (be)[12] only a short distance away. If you _____ (take)[13] the train instead, CO_2 levels _____ (reduce)[14].

3 *Write complete sentences using if-clauses type 2 with would, could or might.*

1 you / think / of the Sahara if you / see / some parts of China today
_____

2 if I / be / a world leader / I / do something / about climate change right now
_____

3 I / can buy / an environmentally-friendly car / if I / earn / more money
_____

4 if we all / use / less energy / we may be able / to stop further environmental damage
_____

5 we / create / less rubbish if we / recycle / more
_____

6 the air / be / much cleaner if we / not fly / so much
_____

4 *Imagine the year is 2100 and climate change has made a lot of the world uninhabitable [unbewohnbar]. Use if-clauses type 3 to complete the sentences.*

1 If CO_2 emissions _____ (not double) every 25 years, it _____ (not put up) temperatures by 6 °C throughout the world.

2 Europe _____ (not hit) by hurricanes every summer if temperatures _____ (remain) normal.

3 If the sea level _____ (not change), some countries _____ (not disappear) under water many years ago.

4 There _____ (be) far fewer problems with CO_2 if more hybrid cars _____ (be built) and if we _____ (introduce) green energy much sooner.

5 If people _____ (burn) less coal and oil, it _____ (may mean) a cooler planet now in 2100.

5 *Translate the missing part of the sentences. Identify the type of if-clause in each case (Type 1, 2, or 3).*

1 It gets hotter *wenn die Temperatur steigt.*
It gets hotter if the temperature rises. (Type: *1*)

2 What will our children think *wenn wir die Atmosphäre nicht schützen?*
_____ (Type:)

3 *Wenn das Eis in Grönland schmilzt*, it'll be possible to look for oil there.
_____ (Type:)

4 It would have helped the atmosphere *wenn man nicht so viel CO_2 produziert hätte.*
_____ (Type:)

5 We could maybe prevent a disaster *wenn wir gegen die Erderwärmung sofort etwas tun würden.*
_____ (Type:)

6 People die as well *wenn Tiere und Pflanzen sterben.*
_____ (Type:)

6 *Spot the problem and correct these sentences.*

1 If we don't do anything soon, it is too late to stop climate change.
_____

2 If we will use our cars less, we cause less pollution.
_____

3 We would go on holiday in Scandinavia, if it were warmer there.
_____

4 If I were you, I will buy a hybrid car.
_____

5 Sylt could have been flooded if sea levels rose dramatically.
_____

6 If the government had enough money, they would do more for the environment last year.
_____

43

15 Relative clauses

A Bestimmende Relativsätze

1 It's often the young **that/who** suffer most.
2 AIDS is a problem **that/which** hits the poor hardest.
3 South Africa is one state **whose** people have been badly affected.
4 Doctors now have drugs (**that/which**) they can use to slow the illness down.
5 They have not found a drug (**that/which**) they can cure the illness **with**. (mehr formell: … **with which** they …)
6 Scientists are doing all (**that**) they can to find a cure.

- Ein bestimmender (= notwendiger) Relativsatz enthält Informationen, ohne die der Hauptsatz nicht verständlich ist. Bei Personen steht *that, who* **(1)**; bei Dingen steht *that, which* **(2, 4, 5)**; *that* benutzt man außerdem nach *all, anything, everything, nothing, something* **(6)**; *whose* (dessen, deren) verwendet man sowohl für Dinge **(3)** wie auch für Personen.
- Sind *that, which, who* Objekt im Relativsatz **(4, 5, 6)**, kann man sie weglassen (= *contact clause*).
- Eine Präposition in einem Relativsatz steht meist am Ende des Relativsatzes **(5)**.

B Nichtbestimmende Relativsätze

1 The continent with the biggest number of AIDS victims is Africa, **which** has well over 20 million.
2 One doctor – **who** developed a new drug and **whose** work is well-known – now says the drug doesn't work.
3 The victims, **who** we must show solidarity with, cannot be cured. (mehr formell: … **with whom** we must …)
4 Sometimes the papers report about a cure, **which** nobody believes is true.

- Ein nichtbestimmender Relativsatz enthält nur Zusatzinformationen und wird immer durch Komma(s) oder Gedankenstrich(e) vom Hauptsatz getrennt. Bei Dingen steht *which, whose* **(1)**; bei Personen steht *who, whose* **(2)**; steht eine Präposition vor *who*, wird im modernen Gebrauch trotzdem *who* geschrieben **(3)**.
- Das Relativpronomen *which* kann sich auf einen ganzen vorhergehenden Satzteil beziehen und entspricht dann „was" im Deutschen **(4)**.

Watch out!

1 In bestimmenden Relativsätzen verwendet man keine Kommas oder Gedankenstriche.
2 *That* steht nie in einem nichtbestimmenden Relativsatz.
3 … *das, was* … = *what* und nicht ~~that, what~~: z.B., Ist **das, was** er gesagt hat wahr? (*Is* **what** *he said true?*)

AIDS

1 *Who or which? Circle the correct relative pronoun.*

1 Nine out of ten young people *who / which* live in the UK do not know enough about AIDS.
2 AIDS is a disease *who / which* kills people at an early age.
3 In the UK, the number of people *who / which* suffer from AIDS is approximately 80,000.
4 AIDS is a problem all over the world but it is Africa *who / which* is worst affected.
5 Eighty thousand people have the disease in Britain, *who / which* seems a relatively small number if you contrast it with Africa.

2 *Fill in that, which, who, whose – but only where it is necessary.*
Sometimes more than one solution is possible.

Anyone _____ [1] has sex knows that their partner might have AIDS. However, the United Nations [*Vereinte Nationen*] has published a study _____ [2] shows that the efforts _____ [3] they have made have not done much to stop the spread of AIDS. According to UN statistics, the number of HIV victims [*Opfer*] has reached 33 million worldwide. The 6,800 victims _____ [4] the UN adds to this figure every day shows that this is a problem _____ [5] will not go away soon. The countries _____ [6] inhabitants are hit hardest and _____ [7] governments are often too poor to improve things are often found in Africa and Asia.
All _____ [8] these governments can really do is hope _____ [9] one day soon somebody will discover a cheap drug _____ [10] will finally beat AIDS.

3 Fill in the correct relative pronouns – where necessary – and the commas.

Some people are HIV positive, _____ ¹ means _____ ² they are infected but are not yet ill. Others have clearly become ill and, once this has happened, they have AIDS _____ ³ always kills the victim in the end. Doctors many of _____ ⁴ have been warning about the disease for years believe that a cure – of _____ ⁵ there are so often false reports in the press – will be found one day.

Southern Africa _____ ⁶ millions of poor people are badly affected is the world's worst area for AIDS. There aren't enough doctors and nurses _____ ⁷ are urgently needed to help the infected population (15%!). But Africa is not the only place where AIDS is a problem. In countries like Vietnam, for example, or Malawi _____ ⁸ area is actually fairly small AIDS is spreading very quickly. In the EU however, the situation is better (only around 70 HIV cases per million). Surprisingly though, the British _____ ⁹ have good doctors and _____ ¹⁰ should understand the dangers have a large number of HIV infections (148.8 per million).

4 Cross out any incorrect relative pronouns and put in commas where necessary.

1 The Africa Foundation *that / which / whose* is financed by a soft drinks company tries to prevent AIDS among the firm's workers.
2 The soft drinks company *who / which / whose* headquarters [*Zentrale*] are in Atlanta, USA was one of the first US firms to give money to fight AIDS in Africa *that / which / what* has helped thousands of people.
3 The $1.5 million *that / which / who* the company recently spent there went to children *whose / that / which* parents had died from AIDS.
4 The region in *whom / which / whose* the foundation spends most money is southern Africa.
5 Dance4Life is an organisation *which / who / what* works with the firm to teach African teenagers about AIDS.
6 Dance4Life and its members without *who / whom / that* the company could achieve little are helping to make a difference in Africa.

5a Translate these sentences.

1 AIDS ist eine Krankheit, deren Ursprung wir kennen.
   _____

2 Es ist ein Problem, das unsere Gesellschaft zerstören kann.
   _____

3 Wir müssen dagegen tun, was wir nur können.
   _____

4 Viele junge Menschen, mit denen Ärzte über AIDS sprechen, verstehen die Gefahr nicht.
   _____

5 Die Stiftung, die schon viel Geld für AIDS-Waisen ausgegeben hat, hat vielen geholfen.
   _____

6 Sex ohne einen Kondom zu benutzen ist ziemlich dumm, was jeder weiß.
   _____

Can you find any contact clause(s) or any non-defining relative clause(s) in your English translations?
Numbers: _____

5b Now translate these sentences into German using a relative pronoun.

1 The projects we finance are all in Africa.

2 Many of the patients they treat are children.

3 The organisation Peter works for is in Kenya.

4 The condom you have in your pocket might be the one you need to save your life.

Focus on ...
Spelling A

Ein häufiges Problem bei der Rechtschreibung liegt bei den Verben. Schreibt man etwa *to stop* in der Vergangenheit (oder in der *-ing* Form) mit einem *p* oder mit zwei *p*? Ein Problem, das bei vielen Verben auftritt.

Quiz

Without using a dictionary, cross out any sentences where you think there is a spelling mistake.

1 I've planed a wonderfull party for tomorrow.
2 I've planned a wonderful party for tomorrow.
3 I've planed a wonderful party for tomorrow.

4 He admitted they had commited the crime.
5 He admited they had commited the crime.
6 He admited they had committed the crime.
7 He admitted they had committed the crime.

8 The patient is sufferring unimaginable pain.
9 The patient is suffering unimaginable pain.
10 The patient is sufering unimaginable pain.

11 They haven't stopped quarrelling all day.
12 They haven't stoped quarelling all day.
13 They haven't stoped quareling all day.

14 The girls prefered to have seperate rooms.
15 The girls preferred to have seperate rooms.
16 The girls preferred to have separate rooms.

17 I've never regretted moving to London.
18 I've never regreted moving to London.

Look at the table and then do exercise 1.

Endkonsonat verdoppelt in:
admit (admi**tt**ed) = zugeben
commit, e.g. a crime (commi**tt**ed) = begehen
control (contro**ll**ed) = beherrschen
dial, e.g. a number (dia**ll**ed) = wählen
fit (fi**tt**ed) = passen
plan (pla**nn**ed) = planen
prefer (prefe**rr**ed) = lieber haben
regret (regre**tt**ed) = bedauern
rob (ro**bb**ed) = berauben
quarrel (quarre**ll**ed) = streiten

Endkonsonant nicht verdoppelt in:
develop (develo**p**ed) = entwickeln
offer (offe**r**ed) = anbieten
profit (profi**t**ed) = profitieren
suffer (suffe**r**ed) = leiden

1 Mark each sentence as right [✓] or wrong [✗] and then correct any wrong sentences. Two sentences are already correct.

1 [ ] They were robed while they were travelling through Florida.
2 [ ] The firm is offerring me the chance to be their official representative in London.
3 [ ] I can't imagine that the new dress fited her.
4 [ ] The West has profited from better relations with countries in the East.
5 [ ] If you don't stop quarreling, you will be disciplined.
6 [ ] I wanted to go to Spain but he prefered Greece.
7 [ ] I've always regretted not visiting my friend in New York.
8 [ ] We're developping a new chocolate bar at work.

Watch out!

Als Faustregel gilt: Ist das vorhergehende *a*, *e*, *i*, *o*, *u* kurz bzw. betont, wird der Endkonsonant meist verdoppelt, z.B. *stop – stopped*.
Die Amerikaner bevorzugen ein *l* bei *traveled*, *dialed*, ...

Test 3

If-clauses (▶ S. 42)

1 *The job candidate*
Write sentences using an if-clause.

1 If Ms Jones / have / a bit more experience / we / offer / her the job immediately [Type 3]
___
2 If the firm / give her the position / she / have to / phone lots of clients in Spain [Type 1]
___
3 Ms Jones / also work in our office in Madrid / if she speak / Spanish [Type 2]
___
4 If we / pay / for a Spanish course / I think / Ms Jones / learn the language in no time [Type 2]
___
5 I'm sure / she be a great secretary / if we / give her the job [Type 1]
___

Reported speech (▶ S. 36)

2 *The financial side of sport*
Look at the speech bubble and then complete the text using reported speech.

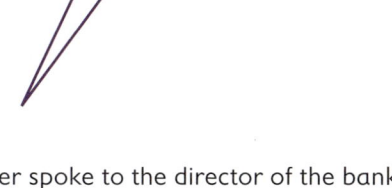

I am delighted that our country has been chosen to host the Olympics. The Games will bring a lot of money to our country and will create thousands of jobs. We do not get many tourists here but the Olympics will change that.

When our reporter spoke to the director of the bank, he said that he _____¹ delighted that _____² country _____³ to host the Olympics. He was certain that the Games _____⁴ a lot of money to _____⁵ country and _____⁶ thousands of jobs. He added that they _____⁷ many tourists _____⁸ but he thought that the Olympics _____⁹ that.

Relative clauses (▶ S. 44)

3 *Smoking*
Cross out any incorrect relative pronouns.

1 There are many countries in Europe *who / which / that / whose* have introduced a smoking ban in public places.
2 The number of people *who / which / that / whose* smoke in Ireland has gone up by about 2% since the smoking ban was introduced there.
3 The world's first smoking ban was introduced by Pope Urban VII in 1590 *who / which / that / whose* threatened to excommunicate anyone who smoked in church.
4 Most people *who / which / that / whose* try to give up smoking fail the first time.
5 Everybody should try to stop smoking, not only people *who / which / that / whose* health is endangered.

Modal auxiliaries (▶ S. 38)

4 *Paralympics*
Fill in the right form of can, must(n't), should(n't) or (not) have to. Sometimes more than one answer is possible.

One _____¹ think that only athletes without disabilities _____² achieve top results. Disabled athletes _____³ compete in the Paralympics, a competition similar to the Olympics. In order to participate in the games, the athletes _____⁴ have the same characteristics as other athletes: skill, determination and a will to win. Most of the disabled athletes are so highly motivated that their coaches _____⁵ tell them to train harder. These athletes' achievements are an inspiration to all disabled people and show them that they _____⁶ pity themselves – they _____⁷ also achieve great things.

47

16 The participle

A Partizip Präsens und Partizip Perfekt nach Konjunktionen

1. Many African goods are produced at low prices **before being sold** in the West at much higher prices. (… before they are sold …)
2. **After earning / Having earned** almost nothing at all last week, this farmer can't feed his family. (After this farmer (had) earned …, he …)
3. **Being** aware of the need to act, certain countries introduced fair trade. (As/Because/Since certain countries were aware …, they …)
4. **Until introduced** in Holland in 1959, the concept of fair trade was unknown in Western economies. (Until the concept of fair trade was introduced …, it …)

- Ein Adverbialsatz (= ein Nebensatz eingeleitet durch eine Konjunktion wie *while*, *after*, usw.) kann verkürzt werden, wenn die Subjekte des Haupt- und Nebensatzes gleich sind. Das Partizip wird bevorzugt in der Schriftsprache verwendet. Wird ein Satz verkürzt, steht das gemeinsame Subjekt meist im Hauptsatz **(1-4)**.
- Steht das Partizip im ersten Satzteil, wird dieser durch ein Komma abgetrennt **(2-4)**.
- In Nebensätzen mit *as*, *because* oder *since* entfällt die Konjunktion bei der Verkürzung **(3)**.
- Das Partizip Perfekt (*past participle*) steht häufig nach *(al)though*, *if*, *unless* [es sei denn], *until*, *when* **(4)**.

B Verschiedene Nebensätze

1. He sold the tea to Fair Deal Ltd, **earning** more than expected. [… wobei er …]
2. He contacted Fair Deal, **hoping** to get a better price. [… und [er] hoffte [dabei] …]
3. **With** big firms **running** things, small farmers have no say. [Da/Weil große Firmen …]

- Ein Partizip Präsens (*present participle*) kann einen Nebensatz ersetzen, der im Deutschen mit „wobei", „dabei", „indem" eingeleitet wird. Die Voraussetzung dafür ist das gleiche Subjekt **(1-2)**.
- Das Partizip nach *with* wird vor allem benutzt, wenn Haupt- und Nebensatz verschiedene Subjekte haben. Dies wird im Deutschen häufig durch „da", „heutzutage / jetzt wo", „seit(dem)", „weil", „wenn" übersetzt **(3)**.

Watch out!

In passiven Sätzen nach Konjunktionen entfällt *being* bei der Verkürzung, z.B. *Unless he is informed*, he can't help. = *Unless informed*, he … . Ausnahmen: *after*, *because*, *before*

Fair trade = fair price

If supermarkets in rich countries sell products from poor countries, like tea, coffee or chocolate, at a higher, fairer price, the poor can make more money from their goods.

1 *Use a present participle or a past participle below. Sometimes you have to put the subject in the main clause.*

1. Before consumers buy tea or coffee, they should consider who earns the most from it.
   Before buying tea or coffee, *consumers* should consider who earns the most from it.
2. Unless growers are given a fair deal, they are certain to stay poor.
   Unless given a fair deal, *growers* are certain to stay poor.
3. When fair trade products were first introduced in Britain, they didn't sell very well.
   _____ in Britain, _____ didn't sell very well.
4. If a coffee grower [Pflanzer] in Peru is offered a fair trade price, he will make about $3 and not $2.40 a day.
   _____ a fair trade price, _____ will make about $3 and not $2.40 a day.
5. People can usually make a profit when they are given the chance.
   People can usually make a profit _____ the chance.
6. As rich countries have become aware of how serious the problem is, they are trying to change things.
   _____ aware of how serious the problem is, _____ are trying to change things.

7 Indian cotton [Baumwolle] producers earned little until they were helped by fair trade programmes.

Indian cotton producers earned little _____ by fair trade programmes.

8 The Fairtrade Foundation expects sales to increase after they have run a new advertising campaign.

_____ a new advertising campaign, the Fairtrade Foundation expects sales to increase.

2 *Join these sentences using a participle. (Remember the comma!)*

1 In the UK there are more than 2,500 fair trade products. They earn about £320 million a year.
In the UK there are more than 2,500 fair trade products, earning about £320 million a year.

2 Fair trade products sold well in Britain last year. It increased sales by 48%.
_____
_____

3 Fair trade offers a small profit for good work. It aims to help the poor.
_____
_____

4 The fair trade system covers many types of products. It includes clothes and furniture.
_____
_____

5 Footballs made in Africa are also part of the fair trade system. They cost around £40 rather than the usual £30.
_____
_____

6 The Fairtrade foundation clearly marks its products. It uses its logo as a label.
_____
_____

7 Many people organise their own events. They promote fair trade in schools and local communities.
_____
_____

8 More and more people recognize the Fairtrade label. This proves the foundation is raising awareness about trade.
_____
_____

3 *The Archbishop [Erzbischof] of York, Dr John Sentamu, thinks people should only buy fair trade chocolate. Complete the sentences below using 'with' and a participle.*

1 *(Da York für seine Schokolade berühmt ist)*
_____, lots of people in the city buy it.

2 *(Seitdem die Anzahl [number] der Schokoladen-Fans in Großbritannien immer größer [bigger and bigger] wird)*
_____, millions have started to take Dr Sentamu seriously.

3 *(Jetzt wo Dr Sentamu viele Anhänger [supporters] hat)*
_____, the food company Nestlé says it'll look at the situation carefully.

4 *(Heutzutage wo keine Firma Kunden verlieren will)*
_____, Nestlé wants to keep its good image.

5 How can we buy non-Fairtrade chocolate
_____
(wenn so viele arme Arbeiter mehr Geld brauchen)?

4 *Translate these sentences using a present or past participle.*

1 Bevor der Kunde den Kaffee kaufte, fragte er nach [about] dem Fairtrade-Zeichen.
2 Während sie in Nigeria lebte, arbeitete sie bei [for] Fair Deal Footballs.
3 „Das ist sehr teuer", sagte er, wobei er auf den Tee zeigte [point to].
4 Da heutzutage so viel Fairtrade-Schokolade gegessen wird, verdienen viele Familien in Ghana mehr als vorher.
5 Der Westen versucht Afrika zu helfen und hofft dabei neue Kunden zu finden.
6 Falls es in Asien produziert wird, wird es sehr billig sein.

17 Forms of 'lassen'

A zulassen

> allow somebody **to do** something
> permit somebody **to do** something
> let somebody **do** something (<u>ohne</u> to!)

1 Don't **allow/permit** rich nations **to do** nothing!
2 **Let** the Third World **have** more money!

● „etwas zulassen/erlauben" wird im Englischen entweder mit *allow/permit somebody to do something* oder mit *let somebody do something* ausgedrückt (1, 2). Im alltäglichen Gebrauch bevorzugt man *let*.

B machen lassen

1 Two countries **had/got** their aid **increased** last year.
2 How **did** they **have/get** it **increased**?

● „Etwas machen lassen" wird im Englischen mit *have/get* + Objekt + Partizip wiedergegeben (1, 2). Meistens ist *get* mit *have* austauschbar. *Get* gilt als weniger formell und wird immer öfter im Alltag benutzt.

C veranlassen

1 Bob Geldof **had** his advisers **inform** him about the situation.
2 He **got** famous bands **to appear** for free.
3 He also **made** governments **change** their attitude.
4 It **made** people **cry** to see the poverty.
5 Governments **have been made to offer** more.

● „Jemanden veranlassen, etwas zu tun" wird mit *have somebody do something* oder *get somebody to do something* wiedergegeben (1, 2), wobei *get* vor allem in der Umgangssprache bevorzugt wird.
● *To make somebody do something* bedeutet zwar auch „veranlassen", jedoch mehr im Sinne von „jemanden dazu zwingen/bringen, etwas zu tun" (3, 4). Im Passiv wird *make* mit *to* + Infinitiv verwendet (5).

Watch out!

Durch Änderung der Wortstellung ergibt sich eine ganz andere Bedeutung:
They had the stadium cleaned after the concert.
= „Sie ließen es sauber machen".
They had cleaned the stadium before the concert.
= „Sie hatten es sauber gemacht".

Live Aid and Bob Geldof

1 *Look at the comments made by fans before the Live Aid Concert at Wembley Stadium, London in 1985. Use the words in brackets to complete the sentences with let or allow/permit … to.*

"I'm here today because I think we can _____ (not allow / people / starve [*verhungern*])¹ in Africa – or anywhere in fact!"

"There are over 70,000 rock fans in this stadium and our message is simple – we will _____ (not let / our government / forget)² Africa's poor."

"You know, if you _____ (permit / politicians / spend)³ money on guns instead of food, then you might as well _____ (let / them / do)⁴ anything they want!"

"This society has failed if it _____ (allow / children / die)⁵ in Sudan and if we _____ (not permit / them / live)⁶ a decent life."

"I've heard that they are going to _____ (let / the BBC / broadcast)⁷ the whole thing worldwide. To 160 countries! Wow!"

"This is a 16-hour music marathon and it's time to make a new world. Why do we _____ (let / the world / continue)⁸ like this? Why do we _____ (allow / a continent / stay)⁹ hungry? We ought to _____ (let / music / change)¹⁰ the planet."

2 *Write sentences using a suitable form of (not) make somebody do something or (not) be made to do something.*

1 The G8 countries must / make / increase / their aid
   _____
   _____

2 How do you / make / them / understand / their obligations/?
   _____
   _____

3 Years ago / it / make / me / cry / to see how little they did / but now / it / make / me / smile / to see things are a bit better at last
   _____
   _____

4 If the G8 members / not make / realize / how terrible the problem is, then the world is lost
   _____
   _____

5 We should feel ashamed that / we / not make / Africans / stop / dying on our TV screens
   _____
   _____

6 If politicians / not make / show / respect for the weak, / then there's no future for any of us
   _____
   _____

3 *Live Aid was the first of many such events. Complete the sentences below with a suitable form of have + object + past participle.*

On 6 to 8 July 2005, the world's eight richest nations – the G8 – met in Scotland. Bob Geldof wanted to do something to raise awareness of poverty in Africa and influence the G8. So he _____ (organise / ten concerts)[1] all over the world on 2 July and called the event "Live 8" to remind people of the "Live Aid" concert in 1985. "Live Aid" was about raising money for Africa, but this time Geldof wanted to _____ (change / international policy)[2] so that Africa's debt could be cancelled. The concerts were all very big – the British concert organisers _____ (put up / a stage)[3] in London's Hyde Park and gave out tickets to 200,000 lucky winners by lottery. The group "Make Poverty History" also organised a demonstration in Scotland, and _____ (produce / white wristbands)[4] for supporters to wear. The events were very popular and on July 8, 2005, the G8 agreed to measures to try and reduce African debt, including _____ (allocate / £28.8 billion pounds)[5] as extra aid.

4 *Translate the sentences using structures from the unit.*

1 Die G8-Länder wurden dazu gezwungen, schnell zu handeln [*act*].
2 Warum lassen wir zu, dass Menschen verhungern?
3 Die Situation brachte mich zum Weinen.
4 Wir müssen den Westen dazu bringen, mehr zu spenden [*donate*].
5 Geldof hat die reichen Nationen veranlasst, mehr Entwicklungshilfe zu geben.
6 Er wird neue Konzerte organisieren lassen.
7 Wie kann man die Welt zwingen, alte Ideen zu ändern?

5 *Spot the problem and correct these sentences. One sentence is already correct.*

1 Geldof and his friend Midge Ure made governments to take action.
   _____
   _____

2 The rich world shouldn't let Africans to die without trying to help them.
   _____
   _____

3 They had famous bands play for free at Wembley in 1985.
   _____
   _____

4 He let the stadium clean directly after the concert.
   _____
   _____

5 You won't get people act differently unless you do something.
   _____
   _____

18 Gerund

A Gerundium (-ing-Form nach Verben und Wendungen)

1 Santosh **suggested starting** his own IT firm.
2 **It's fun making** money, and **there's no denying** it's easy in a globalized world.

- Das Gerundium steht als Objekt nach bestimmten Verben wie: *admit, avoid, begin*, carry on, consider* [erwägen], *continue*, deny* [leugnen], *detest* [verabscheuen], *dislike, enjoy, finish, give up, hate*, can't help* [nicht umhin können], *imagine, intend*, keep (on)* [etwas weiterhin tun], *like*, love*, mind, miss, practise, prefer*, quit* [aufhören], *resist* [widerstehen], *risk, stand* [aushalten], *start*, suggest* **(1)**. * Nach diesen Verben kann auch der Infinitiv (ohne Bedeutungsunterschied) stehen.
- Das Gerundium wird gebraucht nach Ausdrücken wie: *to be busy, it's (no) fun, it's no good/use, there's no point/sense (in), it's (not) worth, there's no (denying, saying, knowing …), to feel like* [Lust haben] **(2)**.

B Gerundium nach Präpositionen

1 Lots of us **dream of working** abroad.
2 He's **keen on finding** a job in Canada.
3 James had **no chance of getting** a job in China.

- Die meisten Verben, die auf eine Präposition außer *to* folgen (geläufige Ausnahme = **look forward to**), stehen in der *-ing*-Form. Die Präposition kann verbunden sein mit einem:

Verb: *believe in, succeed in, specialize in, concentrate on, congratulate somebody on* [gratulieren], *depend on, insist on, decide against, warn somebody against, dream of, suspect somebody of* [verdächtigen], *think of, prevent somebody from, stop somebody from, apologize for, give up* **(1)**.

Adjektiv: *afraid of, proud of* [stolz auf], *sick of, tired of, bad at, good at, crazy about, excited about/at, angry about/at, disappointed about/at, happy about/at, fed up of/with* [etwas satt haben], *fond of* [etwas gerne tun], *used to* [gewöhnt, etwas zu tun], *interested in, keen on* [von etwas begeistert] **(2)**.

Substantiv: *advantage of, chance of, danger of, method of, possibility of, difficulty (in), trouble (in), reason for* **(3)**.

Watch out!
> Es heißt *bad at, good at* (**nicht** *bad in, good in*); es heißt *possibility of* (**nicht** *possibility to*)!

Globalization

The South Indian city of Bangalore is now the Silicon Valley of Asia and the country plays a leading part in globalization.

1 *Fill in the gerunds. Then circle the two verbs which can also take the infinitive.*

A few years ago most Europeans had never considered _____ (work)[1] in India but times have changed. Rick Haill, an IT expert, began _____ (send off)[2] applications to firms in India after his friend, Santosh, suggested _____ (try)[3] his luck in Bangalore. At first, Rick couldn't imagine _____ (live)[4] in such a hot place and _____ (travel)[5] to his office in the monsoon! But now he loves his job so much he's learning Hindi!

Santosh also works in Bangalore and finished _____ (design)[6] his own web-based travel firm a while ago. Business is booming now, but when he started _____ (sell)[7] online holidays, it took a while to make money and he risked _____ (lose)[8] everything.

2 *Rewrite these sentences using the gerund.*

Rick said:

1 "I'm not sure it would be nice to work in Bangalore."
   Rick couldn't imagine **working in Bangalore**.

2 "I was scared about moving to India at first."
   He admitted _____.

52

3 "I had my first Hindi class last Thursday."

He started _____.

4 "I don't think about moving back to Britain anymore."

He has given up _____.

Santosh said:

5 "I'd rather work for myself in my own business than work for someone else".

Santosh prefers _____.

6 "I might start a second business soon."

He is considering _____.

3 Circle the gerund with the correct preposition.

Mike Modesto (17) from LA wanted to go to college and was interested *for improving / in improving*¹ his grades. He dreamed *of attending / from attending*² the University of California, but he had problems with maths. Geometry was okay but he wasn't good *at solving / in solving*³ algebra problems. His mother was so fed up *in listening / of listening*⁴ to her son complain about his school work that she insisted *on contacting / at contacting*⁵ TutorVision, an e-tutoring service in Bangalore which charged just $2.85 per hour. Both mother and son believe *at doing / in doing*⁶ their best and TutorVision seemed a much better idea than paying $100 per hour in the USA! So a surprising result of globalization – it prevented Mike *from failing / in failing*⁷ maths! In fact, last month Mike's family was able to congratulate him *on becoming / to becoming*⁸ top of his class and getting a place at his dream university.

4 Translate the words in brackets using a gerund with the correct phrase.

1 _____ that India has a big part to play in globalization. (*Es läßt sich nicht leugnen* …)

2 _____ to stop globalization. (*Es hat keinen Sinn zu versuchen* …)

3 Nowadays _____ a job in the IT sector in India. (… *es lohnt sich zu suchen* …)

4 India is the world's biggest exporter of IT services, and that's why many Europeans _____ there. (… *haben Lust … zu arbeiten*…)

5 Many employees say _____ software in Bangalore. (…*es macht Spaß … zu entwickeln* …)

6 _____ if the future of the IT industry lies in Asia, not in the USA. (*Man kann nicht wissen* …)

5 Spot the problem and correct these sentences.

1 Many rich nations are busy with investing abroad.
   _____

2 Some people dislike to have to live in a globalized world.
   _____

3 Nowadays everybody is used to buy goods from abroad.
   _____

4 I'd suggest to try your luck in India.
   _____

5 Is it really worth to get a tutor from Bangalore?
   _____

6 I'm thinking of to learn maths by e-tutoring.
   _____

7 Sue isn't good in making a good impression at interviews.
   _____

8 Our family could never imagine to leave Britain for India.
   _____

6 Some toys from China have caused big problems in Europe and the USA. Translate these sentences with a gerund.
Sometimes there may be more than one solution.

1 Verbraucher [*consumers*] in den USA wurden davor gewarnt, Spielzeuge aus China zu kaufen.
2 Einige US-Firmen sind darauf spezialisiert, solche Produkte zu importieren.
3 Gibt es die Möglichkeit, sie in Europa zu produzieren?
4 Eltern müssen ihre Kinder daran hindern, solche Spielzeuge zu benutzen.
5 Viele Eltern bestehen darauf, ihr Geld zurückzubekommen [*get back*].
6 Firmen in China haben es satt, kritisiert zu werden.
7 Die Wirtschaft [*economy*] hängt davon ab, Waren von guter Qualität zu exportieren.
8 Gute Qualität ist die beste Methode neue Kunden zu gewinnen [*gain*].

19 Gerund and infinitive

A Bedeutungsunterschiede

🟧 Die Verben *remember*, *forget*, *go on*, *stop*, *try* und *regret* haben unterschiedliche Bedeutungen, je nachdem ob ein Gerundium oder ein Infinitiv folgt.

remember to do sth = daran denken, etwas zu tun
Please remember to buy that new diet book.
remember doing sth = sich erinnern, etwas getan zu haben
Most of us can remember eating a bit too much as kids.

forget to do sth = vergessen, etwas zu tun
She forgot to buy some fruit.
forget doing sth = vergessen, etwas getan zu haben
How could I forget enjoying those wonderful cakes in Austria?

go on to do sth = etwas Anderes als Nächstes tun
He went on to explain the problems eating too much can cause.
go on doing sth = etwas weiterhin tun
He went on talking about food for hours.

stop to do sth = anhalten, um etwas (Anderes) zu tun
Shall we stop to get a pizza here?
stop doing sth = aufhören, etwas zu tun
Once I start, I just can't stop eating!

try to do sth = sich bemühen, etwas zu tun
Mike tries to avoid fast food and cola.
try doing sth = etwas (aus)probieren
Why don't you try drinking fruit juice instead?

regret to do sth = etwas bedauern
I regret to tell you that you've put on weight.
regret doing sth = etwas bereuen
I regret eating that chocolate cake.

B Infinitiv, nicht Gerundium

1 I **hope to lose** some weight before my holiday next year.
2 I **would love to stop** eating so much!

🟧 Nach einigen gängigen Verben steht anstelle des Gerundiums der Infinitiv. Wie beim Gerundium (s. Seite 52) sind diese Kombinationen feststehend und können daher auswendig gelernt werden: *afford*, *agree*, *attempt* [versuchen], *choose*, *consider* [halten für], *dare* [wagen], *decide*, *expect*, *fail* [unterlassen; es nicht schaffen], *help*, *hope*, *learn*, *manage* [schaffen], *offer*, *plan*, *promise*, *refuse*, *seem*, *wish* **(1)**.
🟧 Bei *would hate*, *would like*, *would love*, *would prefer* folgt immer der Infinitiv **(2)**.

I'm too fat!

1 *Translate the missing sentence parts below with a gerund or infinitive. Use remember, forget, go on, stop or try.*

1 *Hamish (42) aus Glasgow **erinnert sich**, wie er in einem Land von relativ schlanken Menschen **aufwuchs**.*

Hamish (42) from Glasgow _____ in a country of relatively slim people.

2 *Zu seiner übergewichtigen Tochter Sheila (16) muss er aber immer wieder sagen: „**Denke bitte daran**, weniger Kalorien zu essen."*

But he has to tell his overweight daughter Shelia (16) again and again: "_____ fewer calories."

3 *Wir **haben nicht vergessen**, wie wir zum ersten Mal einen Bericht über Fettsucht bei Teenagern **lasen**.*

We _____ a report about obesity among teenagers for the first time.

4 *Leider **habe ich vergessen**, mehr Obst zu **kaufen**.*

Unfortunately _____ more fruit.

5 *Wer schlank bleiben will, soll einfach **weiterhin** gesund **essen**.*

Anyone who wants to stay slim should simply _____ healthily.

6 *Die Ernährungswissenschaftlerin **erklärte** mir als **Nächstes** einen neuen Niedrig-Kalorien-Plan.*

The dietician _____ a new low-calorie plan to me.

7 *Menschen, die **nicht aufhören können**, ungesund **zu leben**, sterben oft früher.*

People who _____ unhealthily often die earlier.

8 *Die Hamiltons **hielten an**, um beim neuen Health-Food-Drive-In **zu essen**.*

The Hamiltons _____ at the new health food drive-in.

9 *Eric **bemüht sich**, weniger Fastfood **zu essen**.*

Eric _____ less fast food.

10 *Du solltest **probieren**, mehr Obst **zu essen**.*

You should _____ more fruit.

2 Spot the problem and correct the wrong sentences. One sentence is already correct.

1. Experts consider obesity being the cause of many illnesses.
2. Teenagers who attempt going on a diet can't normally keep to it.
3. Parents can't afford to admit that they themselves are too fat!
4. Many young girls wish becoming slim at any price.
5. People on diets often regret to eat unhealthy food.
6. Statistically, young people who eat very small amounts can expect developing anorexia.
7. Another problem is bulimia, where people more or less refuse stopping eating.
8. Many people with eating disorders don't manage changing their lifestyle and so die young.

3 Gerund, infinitive or both? Complete the text with the words in brackets.

Should 'size zero' models be banned?

In 2006, the organizers of Madrid Fashion Week were the first to decide _____ (ban)[1] seriously underweight models. They agreed _____ (introduce)[2] the new regulations after talks with the local government, who wanted _____ (give)[3] young people a more positive and healthy body image.

Since then, many fashion events have also begun _____ (limit)[4] their use of underweight models. Brazil, however, decided against _____ (control)[5] the weight of their models and instead gave young models lessons in healthy eating.

Of course, not everyone is in favour of banning 'size zero' models. Many see this as just another form of discrimination. As one thin model said, "No one would dream of _____ (say)[6] that fat models can't work at a fashion show. So why should it be any different for us?"

4 Rewrite these sentences using the gerund or an infinitive. The verbs in the box will help you.

afford • be good at • decide • enjoy • promise • suggest

1. Mark: "We could try that new restaurant maybe?"

   Mark suggested trying that new restaurant.

2. I've made a decision: I'm going to exercise more.

3. I go to the gym every week. I enjoy it.

4. Jane made a promise: "I'm going to eat less chocolate."

5. Matt plays football. He's good at it.

6. I can't join a gym. It costs too much.

5 Translate these sentences using either a gerund or an infinitive.

1. Niemand erwartet, dass du mehr als 10 Kilo abnimmst.
2. Sie ist daran gewöhnt, ohne Frühstück in die Schule zu gehen.
3. Ich würde vorschlagen, nächste Woche einen Fitnesskurs zu beginnen.
4. Wir würden lieber Fleisch als Gemüse essen.
5. Er beabsichtigt, eine neue Diät auszuprobieren.
6. Ich habe keine Lust, jeden Tag immer dicker zu werden.
7. Wird sie es schaffen in Zukunft auf ihre tägliche Schokolade zu verzichten [do without]?
8. Ich hasse es, hungrig ins Bett zu gehen.

It's not wise to eat to one's full capacity.

20 Question tags

1 The Olympic Games **are** too expensive, **aren't they**?
2 You **can't** get tickets for the opening ceremony, **can you**?
3 The Games **have** often been influenced by politics, **haven't they**?
4 More athletes **will** be tested for drugs, **won't they**?
5 Most athletes **live** in the Olympic village, **don't they**?
6 He **doesn't like** the swimming events, **does he**?
7 They **went** to the hockey field, **didn't they**?
8 Most athletes **have** breakfast in the Olympic village, **don't they**?
9 The state **has to** invest a lot of money in new stadiums, **doesn't it**?
10 **Let's** try to get tickets for the final, **shall we**?

- Wird das Frageanhängsel als Informationsfrage benutzt, weil man sich nicht sicher ist oder nicht weiß, ob etwas wahr ist, so steigt die Stimme.
- Wird das Frageanhängsel als Aufforderung zur Zustimmung des Gesprächspartners benutzt, so fällt die Stimme.
- Im Deutschen wird das Frageanhängsel oft mit „nicht wahr", „oder" und „stimmt's" wiedergegeben.

- Das Subjekt des Hauptsatzes entspricht dem Subjekt des Frageanhängsels **(1-9)**.
- Alle Formen von *be*, *can*, *have* und *will* haben ihre entsprechenden Formen auch im Frageanhängsel **(1-4)**.
- Wenn Gegenwarts- und Vergangenheitsformen von Vollverben im Aussagesatz vorkommen, so werden sie im Frageanhängsel mit *do/don't*, *does/doesn't* oder *did/didn't* wieder aufgenommen **(5-7)**.
- Ist eine Aussage bejahend, wird das Frageanhängsel verneint **(1, 3, 4, 5, 7, 8, 9)**.
- Ist eine Aussage verneinend, wird das Frageanhängsel bejaht **(2, 6)**.
- Nach Vorschlägen mit *let's,* wird das Frageanhängsel *shall we* benutzt **(10)**.

Watch out!

Bei *have* mit Zusammensetzungen wie *have lunch*, *a shower*, ... und *have to* [müssen] wird im Frageanhängsel eine Form von *do* benutzt **(8, 9)**.

The Olympic Games

1 *Fill in the correct question tags.*

1 Ancient Greece held the first Olympic Games, _____?
2 Women weren't allowed to take part, _____?
3 The IOC selects a city for the Olympic Games, _____?
4 The Games will bring a lot of money and create jobs, _____?
5 We can't afford not to have the Games, _____?
6 The estimated price of the Games has doubled from the original price, _____?
7 Athletes who have no chance of winning just have a good time, _____?
8 There is too much drug abuse, _____?
9 There aren't enough tickets for Olympic events, _____?
10 We have to be better prepared for the Games, _____?

2 *Translate these questions using question tags.*

1 Lasst uns zur Eröffnungsfeier gehen, oder?
_____
_____, _____?

2 Wir sehen uns beim Spiel nächste Woche, nicht wahr?
_____
_____, _____?

3 Die Karten waren echt teuer, nicht wahr?
_____
_____, _____?

4 Du kannst morgen nicht mitkommen, oder?
_____
_____, _____?

Focus on ...
Spelling B

Quiz

Without using a dictionary, cross out any sentences where you think there is a spelling mistake.

1. I'll send a telegramm to his appartment in New York.
2. I'll send a telegram to his appartment in New York.
3. I'll send a telegram to his apartment in New York.

4. The goverment must do more for the enviroment.
5. The government must do more for the enviromnent.
6. The government must do more for the environment.
7. The governmnent must do more for the environment.

8. There's an address on the cassette.
9. There's an address on the casette.
10. There's an adress on the cassette.

11. It was the eighth day of the twelvth month.
12. It was the eightht day of the twelfth month.
13. It was the eighth day of the twelfth month.

14. Most germans know a few english words.
15. Most Germans know a few English words.
16. Most Germans know a few english words.

17. The lack of succes is disappointing.
18. The lack of sucess is disappointing.
19. The lack of success is disappointing.
20. The lack of success is dissappointing.
21. The lack of success is dissapointing.

22. Your help won't be neccesary.
23. Your help won't be necessary.
24. Your help won't be nesessary.

Look at the following information (A-D) and then do exercise 1.

A Konsonanten: Einer oder zwei?

ein Konsonant	zwei Konsonanten
apartment = Wohnung	actually = tatsächlich
career = Karriere	annoy = ärgern
emigrate = auswandern	commit = (ein Verbrechen) begehen
metal = Metall	glass = Glas
model = Modell	gradually = allmählich
rebel = Rebell	immigrate = einwandern
telegram = telegramm	scissors = (eine) Schere
einer plus zwei	**zwei plus zwei**
disappear = verschwinden	access = Zugang
disappoint = enttäuschen	accommodation = Unterkunft
necessary = notwendig	address = Adresse, Anschrift
parallel = parallel	assassinate = ermorden
	cassette = Kassette
	success = Erfolg

B Konsonanten: Weitere Tücken

belief (to believe = glauben)	height = Höhe
life (to live = leben)	straight = gerade
proof (to prove = beweisen)	environment = Umwelt
safe = sicher (to save = sparen; retten)	government = Regierung
where = wo	
whether = ob	

C Zahlen

four	five	eight	twelve
fourteen	fifteen	eighteen	
forty	fifty	eighty	
fourth	fifth	eighth	twelfth

D Groß oder klein?

Folgende Wörter werden immer **groß** geschrieben:
- Land, Leute, Sprache und Staatsangehörigkeit: **E**ngland, **E**nglish, **A**merican, **D**utch, **G**erman, usw.
- Religionen: **C**atholic (Katholik/in; katholisch), **J**ewish (jüdisch), **M**uslim (Moslem; muslimisch), usw.
- Tage: on **M**onday(s) (am Montag; montags), on **T**uesdays (am Dienstag, dienstags), usw.

1 Translate the words in brackets.

1. How many _____ (Rebellen) were able to escape?
2. What's the difference between 'to _____' (auswandern) and 'to _____' (einwandern)?
3. Her _____ (Karriere) was a great _____ (Erfolg).

▶▶▶

4 John F. Kennedy was _____ (ermordet) in 1963. Why would anybody _____ (begehen) such a crime?

5 Lines which are _____ (parallel) must also be _____ (gerade).

6 I'm not sure _____ (ob) I can spell the words '_____' (Glaube) and '_____' (Beweis).

7 What's _____ (vierzehn) plus _____ (vierzig)?

8 Is that a _____ (jüdische) or a _____ (muslimische) custom?

Look at the following information (E-G) and then do exercise 2.

E -ise oder -ize?

Häufig ist die Endung -ise mit -ize austauschbar (realise v. realize). Heutzutage wird jedoch bevorzugt -ize benutzt.

-ize (oft -ieren im Dt.)	-ise ist unveränderlich in:
civilize = zivilisieren criticize = kritisieren emphasize = betonen organize = organisieren recognize = erkennen symbolize = symbolisieren	advertise = Reklame machen advise = (be)raten (aber: advice = Ratschlag) exercise = Übung; üben practise = üben (aber: practice = Übung/Brauch und AE) supervise = beaufsichtigen surprise = überraschen televise = im Fernsehen übertragen

F Ein Wort oder mehrere Wörter?

another	all right
cannot	in spite of
despite	no one
someone	

G Bindestriche

- Bei den Vorsilben **anti**-British, **ex**-policeman, **pro**-American, **self**-confidence ist ein Bindestrich immer notwendig sowie bei Zahlen (thirty-two, sixty-five, usw.).
- Merken Sie sich folgende Zusammensetzungen: *a two-year-old child, a fifty-pound note, a well-known author* (immer **mit** Bindestrich vor einem Substantiv). Aber *he is well known / he is two years old*.
- Im Englischen werden Zusammensetzungen aus Abkürzungen und Substantiven in der Regel ohne Bindestrich geschrieben: *UN troops, NATO conference*. Aber: *A-Level* (etwa: Abitur, BE).

2 Correct these sentences.

1 The Chinese televized an antibritish programme.
2 John has no selfconfidence inspite of the fact that he's a well known singer.
3 He's irish, sixty five years old and an ex-policeman.
4 People were surprised, even anoyed to hear that sort of advise from the director, but noone realised that he was actualy joking.
5 I can not seriously belief that an other ten mile walk at the weekend will help me to lose more weight, although I certainly need more exercize.
6 You have been chosen to attend the UN-conference in Berlin as part of the UK-delegation.

Look at the following information (H-I) and then do exercises 3 and 4.

H Vokale mit Tücken

[a]	[ie]
cal**a**endar = Kalender coc**oa** = Kakao rep**ea**t = wiederholen sep**a**rate = getrennt	ch**ie**f = Häuptling n**ie**ce = Nichte th**ie**f = Dieb
[ei] after [c]	**[e]**
c**ei**ling = Decke rec**ei**ve = empfangen rec**ei**pt = Quittung; Erhalt	aggr**e**ssive = aggresiv b**ei**ng (nur ein ‚e') employ**ee** = Arbeitnehmer magaz**i**ne = Zeitschrift medicin**e** = Medizin satell**i**te = Satellit

I … und noch ein paar Vokalen zum "drüberstolpern".

can**oe** = Kanu
che**que** = Scheck
ch**oi**r = Chor
colle**ague** = Kollege/-in
dialo**gue** = Dialog
parl**ia**ment = Parlament
poisono**us** = giftig
pron**u**nciation (> pron**ou**nce) = Aussprache
q**ueue** = (Warte-)Schlange; Schlange stehen
religi**ous** = religiös

3 Translate the missing parts of the sentences.

1. Laut dem Kalender ist morgen der 25. Juli.
   _____ it's the 25 July tomorrow.

2. Zwei meiner Kollegen singen im Chor.
   _____ sing _____ .

3. Es ist nur Medizin – es ist nichts Giftiges!
   It's only _____ – it's nothing _____ !

4. Der Dieb stahl zwei Schecks.
   _____ stole _____ .

5. Die Gäste saßen an getrennten Tischen.
   The guests sat at _____ .

4 Translate the following words.

1. Kanu _____
2. Decke _____
3. empfangen _____
4. Aussprache _____
5. Schlange stehen _____
6. Kakao _____
7. Nichte _____
8. Arbeitnehmer _____

Look at the following information (J-L) and then do exercise 5.

J -able oder -ible?

-able (nach Konsonanten und immer nach Vokalen – Vorsicht nach ‚e')	-ible (weniger gebräuchlich – meistens nach 's')
readable = lesenswert uncomfortable = unbequem reliable (> to rely) = zuverlässig admirable (> to admire) = bewundernswert recyclable (> to recycle) = wiederverwendbar unimaginable (> to imagine) = unvorstellbar valuable (> to value) = wertvoll Aber: unpronounceable = unaussprechbar	edible = essbar responsible = verantwortlich visible = sichtbar

K -ant oder -ent?

assistant = Assistent/in	independent = unabhängig
confident = (selbst)sicher	violent = gewalttätig
efficient = tüchtig	

L -ll oder -l?

Nur ein ‚l' in der Endung -ful
beautiful = (wunder)schön careful = sorgfältig successful = erfolgreich wonderful = wunderbar Aber: till / until = bis

5 Translate the following sentences.

1. Das Wort ist fast unaussprechbar.
   _____

2. Der neue Assistent ist zuverlässig, selbstsicher und tüchtig.
   _____

3. Carrie ist wunderschön und erfolgreich.
   _____

4. Warte bis ich komme.
   _____

5. Der Plan ist bewundernswert, aber unvorstellbar. Bist du dafür verantwortlich?
   _____

It's cold in my room. Can I get another ceiling?

Test 4

The participle (▶ S. 48)

1 *Keep on rapping!*
Translate these sentences about a British rapper using a present or a past participle. Watch out for the subject and 'with'.

1 (*Bevor Johno als Sänger berühmt wurde*) **Before becoming famous as a singer, Johno** worked in Liverpool clubs.

2 He got a contract with EGT Records (*nachdem er seine erste CD gemacht hatte*) _____
_____ .

3 (*Seitdem die Absatzzahlen [sales figures] seiner CDs so schnell steigen*) _____
he is one of Britain's richest rappers.

4 (*Jetzt wo Rap immer beliebter wird*) _____
_____ entertainers like Johno are huge stars.

5 (*Bis Johno von EGT entdeckt wurde*) _____
_____ had spent 6 months in jail.

6 (*Falls seine neue CD zu Weihnachten vermarktet [market] wird*) _____
_____ should be a great success.

Forms of 'lassen' (▶ S. 50)

2 *Pop divas*
Are these sentences about a pop star getting ready for a concert right [✓] or wrong [✗]? Correct the wrong sentences.

1 [ ] She let her hair and make-up do by her beautician.
_____

2 [ ] She got her assistant to find her a new dress for the show.
_____

3 [ ] She made the organisers to buy her special bottled water.
_____

4 [ ] She wouldn't let anyone to talk to her before the concert.
_____

5 [ ] The concert organisers allowed her to smoke while she was getting ready.
_____

Gerund (▶ S. 52)

3 *Buying a car*
Rewrite these sentences using the gerund and the correct preposition.

1 I've wanted to buy a Ferrari since I was a child.
I've dreamed **of buying a Ferrari since I was a child.**

2 Maybe I'll buy an environmentally-friendly car.
I'm thinking _____

3 I'd like to find out more about hybrid cars.
I'm interested _____

4 I'm not going to get a car with a sun roof.
I've decided _____

5 I might buy my friend's old car. He said I could buy it.
There's the possibility _____

6 I can't wait to drive my new car for the first time.
I'm excited _____

Gerund and infinitive (▶ S. 54)

4 *Planning a birthday party*
Fill in the gaps using a gerund or an infinitve.

A What shall I do for my birthday?

B Well, what do you like _____ ¹ (do)?

A Hm, I really enjoy _____ ² (dance) so maybe I could have a party.

B That sounds like a good idea. I could try _____ ³ (book) a room in the village hall for you and we could consider _____ ⁴ (hire) a DJ.

A That sounds great! I would love _____ ⁵ (invite) my friends to something like that.

B Great. Well I'll help _____ ⁶ (organize) it if you like.

A Thank you. You know I'm not good at _____ ⁷ (plan) things!

B Fine. I think it's fun _____ ⁸ (arrange) parties. First of all I suggest _____ ⁹ (buy) food and drink from the local supermarket. Then we have to start _____ ¹⁰ (think about) who to invite …

Phrasal verbs

1 Last week he **gave up** smoking for the third time.
2 Last week he **gave** smoking **up** for the third time.
3 Last week he **gave** it **up** for the third time.

Ein *phrasal verb* besteht aus einem Verb (z.B. *give*) und einem Adverb (z.B. *up*). Ist das Objekt eines *phrasal verbs* ein Substantiv (z.B. *smoking*), so kann es entweder direkt hinter dem Adverb (**1**) oder zwischen Verb und Adverb stehen (**2**) – ein Pronomen (z.B. *it*) dagegen muss zwischen Verb und Adverb stehen (**3**).

The car will **break down** if it has no oil. [*eine Panne haben*]

Why should women **bring up** (raise) children alone? [*erziehen*]

Mary **fell down / over** and broke her arm. [*hin-/umfallen*]

You have to **fill in / out** (complete) a form to get a passport. [*ausfüllen*]

You can **find out** their number from the phone book. [*herausfinden*]

Two more prisoners **got away** (escaped) last night. [*entkommen*]

Don't **get in / on** (board) the train until it stops. [*einsteigen*]

We **got off / out of** the bus in the town centre. [*aussteigen*]

Does Jack always **get up** so early? [*aufstehen*]

She **gave away** £10,000 when she won the lottery. [*verschenken*]

The doctor told him to **give up** (stop) smoking. [*aufgeben*]

Well, **go on** (continue). What did she say? [*weitermachen*]

Surely Ann doesn't want to **go out** with that awful man! [*ausgehen*]

I haven't lived here long. I **grew up** (was raised) in Norfolk. [*aufwachsen*]

I asked him to stop but he just **kept on** (continued). [*weitermachen*]

Don't do all the questions. **Leave out** (Omit) the last three. [*auslassen*]

Mary must **look after** (mind) her brother. [*sich kümmern um*]

Have you seen the dog? I've **looked for** him everywhere. [*suchen*]

I always **look forward to** Jill's parties. They're fun. [*sich freuen auf*]

Look out (Pay attention)! That car isn't going to stop. [*aufpassen*]

Look up (Find) the words in your dictionary. [*nachschlagen*]

Please **pick up** (collect) the rubbish and take it away. [*aufheben*]

Please **put away** your books before going home. [*wegräumen*]

It's cold today. I'd **put on** (wear) a thicker pullover. [*anziehen*]

Can you **speak up** (speak louder)? I can't hear you. [*lauter sprechen*]

Can I **stay up** and watch the late night movie? [*aufbleiben*]

Did you **switch / turn off** the coffee machine? [*ausschalten*]

Switch / turn on the television, please. (*an- / einschalten*)

Take off (remove) your coat and **sit down**. [*ausziehen, setzen*]

Jane's plane **takes off** (leaves) at three o'clock. [*starten*]

Always **try on** shoes before you buy them. [*anprobieren*]

I was so tired that I didn't **wake up** for ten hours. [*aufwachen*]

Did you leave the plates for me to **wash up**? [*abwaschen, spülen*]

Can you **work out** (calculate) 2.7 + 0.3 × 6? [*ausrechnen*]

Please **write down** what I say. I won't say it again. [*aufschreiben*]

Complete the phrasal verbs in these sentences.

1 Don't stop. Please go _____ .

2 I'm looking _____ my holiday.

3 She'll look _____ the house when I'm away.

4 I'm on a diet so I've given _____ chocolate.

5 I need to get _____ early for school tomorrow.

6 Don't put that book _____ – I'm using it!

Grammatikbegriffe

englisch	deutsch	Beispiel / Erklärung
active	Aktiv	Jim **paid** the bill. (vgl. dazu auch Passiv)
adjectives	Eigenschaftswörter	efficient, economical, smooth, …
adverbs	Adverbien / Umstandswörter	Sie drücken aus, **wann**, **wo** und **wie** etwas geschieht.
auxiliaries	Hilfsverben	Sie werden im Zusammenhang mit anderen Verben benutzt, um Zeiten oder Fragen zu bilden.
clause	Nebensatz	Er bestimmt die Umstände eines Hauptsatzes. I'd like a car like that **because it's very fast**.

comparison
    comparative
    superlative
	Steigerung
	    1. Steigerung
	    2. Steigerung
		
		fast**er**, **more** beautiful
		fast**est**, **most** beautiful

conjunctions	Konjunktionen	Wörter, die Haupt- und Nebensätze miteinander verbinden: when, because, (al)though, …
countable	zählbar	five books, one car, lots of people, …

future (tense)
    will future
    going to future
    simple present
    present continuous
    future continuous
    future perfect
	Zukunft	There **will be** too many cars in the future.
		It**'s going to rain** soon.
		The train **leaves** at ten o'clock.
		I**'m having** a party next weekend.
		This time next week I**'ll be lying** on the beach.
		Tomorrow I**'ll have finished** the report.

if-clauses	Bedingungssätze	Sätze mit **if** (= wenn)
infinitive	Grundform des Verbs	Die Form des Verbs, die man im Wörterbuch findet; ohne Endungen, z. B. drive, watch; oft davor to.
modal auxiliaries	Modalverben	can, could, should, may, might, …
passive	Passiv	The bill **was paid** (by Jim). (vgl. dazu Aktiv)

past (tense)
    simple past
    past continuous
	Vergangenheit
	    einfache …
	    Verlaufsform der …
		
		answer ▶ answered, go ▶ went
		Betty **was reading** when he came in.

past participle	Partizip Perfekt / -ed form	Einige Verben (wie been, brought, taken) bilden das past participle nicht auf -ed; man verwendet dennoch den Begriff '-ed form'

present (tense)
    simple present
    present continuous
	Gegenwart
	    einfache …
	    Verlaufsform der …
		
		John **gets up** at 7 o'clock. (= immer)
		Look, **it's raining**. (= gerade)

present perfect	Perfekt	Besagt, dass etwas zwar in der Vergangenheit angefangen hat, jedoch schließt die Gegenwart mit ein. She **has** already **eaten**. (Und deswegen hat sie keinen Hunger mehr.)
present perfect continuous	Verlaufsform des Perfekts	vgl. present perfect, nur hier wird die Zeitdauer betont. She **has been smoking** for one hour.
quantifiers	Mengenbezeichnungen	some, any, much, many, (a) few, …
question tag	angehängte Kurzfrage	It's expensive, **isn't it?**
relative pronoun / clause	Relativpronomen/-satz	who, which, that, … I've got a book **which might interest you**.
reported speech	indirekte Rede	Jill said that Jack was ill.
third person singular	dritte Person Einzahl	he, she, it, Leslie, …
uncountable	nicht zählbar	sugar, money, petrol, …

verbs
    verb + -ing form
    verb + object + infinitive
    phrasal verbs
    prepositional verbs
	Verben
	    + -ing-Form
	    … + Objekt + Infinitiv
	    … + Adverbien
	    … + Präpositionen
		to work, to write, to …
		He **finished writing** the report.
		I **told him to go**.
		
		to carry **out**, to close **down**, …
		to approve **of**, to depend **on**, …

Zeitentabelle

Aktiv

Zeiten	Formen		Bildung	Deutsch
Present				
	simple	I work	Infinitiv	ich arbeite
	continuous	I am working	Formen von be + Verb + ing	ich arbeite gerade
Past				
	simple	I worked	-ed form des Verbs	ich arbeitete
	continuous	I was working	Vergangenheit von be + Infinitiv + ing	ich arbeitete gerade
Present perfect				
	simple	I have worked	have/has + 3. Form des Verbs	ich habe gearbeitet
	continuous	I have been working	have/has been + Infinitiv + ing	ich habe gerade gearbeitet/ ich arbeite schon seit …
Past perfect				
	simple	I had worked	had + 3. Form des Verbs	ich hatte gearbeitet
	continuous	I had been working	had been + Infinitiv + ing	ich hatte gerade gearbeitet
Future				
	simple	I will work	will + Infinitiv	ich werde arbeiten
	continuous	I will be working	will be + Infinitiv + ing	ich werde gerade arbeiten
	perfect	I will have worked	will + have + 3. Form des Verbs	ich werde gearbeitet haben
Conditional				
	simple	I would work	would + Infinitiv	ich würde arbeiten
	continuous	I would be working	would be + Infinitiv + ing	ich würde gerade arbeiten
Conditional perfect				
	simple	I would have worked	would have + 3. Form des Verbs	ich würde gearbeitet haben
	continuous	I would have been working	would have been + Infinitiv + ing	ich würde gerade gearbeitet haben

Passiv

Zeiten	Formen		Bildung	Deutsch
Present				
	simple	I am asked	Form von be + 3. Form des Verbs	ich werde gefragt
	continuous	I am being asked	Form von be + 3. Form des Verbs	ich werde gerade gefragt
Past				
	simple	I was asked	Vergangenheit von be + 3. Form des Verbs	ich wurde gefragt
	continuous	I was being asked	Vergangenheit von be + being + 3. Form des Verb	ich wurde gerade gefragt
Present perfect				
		I have been asked	have/has been + 3. Form des Verbs	ich bin gefragt worden
Past perfect				
		I had been asked	had been + 3. Form des Verbs	ich war gefragt worden
Future				
	simple	I will be asked	will be + 3. Form des Verbs	ich werde gefragt werden
	continuous	I will be being asked	will be being + 3. Form des Verbs	ich werde gerade gefragt werden
	perfect	I will have been asked	will have been + 3. Form des Verbs	ich werde gefragt worden sein
Conditional				
		I would be asked	would be + 3. Form des Verbs	ich würde gefragt werden
Conditional perfect				
		I would have been asked	would have been + 3. Form des Verbs	ich würde gefragt worden sein

Unregelmäßige Verben

Grundform	Vergangenheit	3. Form	Bedeutung
be	was/were	been	sein
become	became	become	werden
begin	began	begun	anfangen
bring	brought	brought	bringen
build	built	built	bauen
buy	bought	bought	kaufen
catch	caught	caught	fangen
come	came	come	kommen
cost	cost	cost	kosten
do	did	done	tun, machen, erledigen
draw	drew	drawn	zeichnen
dream	dreamt/dreamed	dreamt/dreamed	träumen
drink	drank	drunk	trinken, saufen
drive	drove	driven	fahren
eat	ate	eaten	essen, fressen
feel	felt	felt	sich fühlen
find	found	found	finden
fly	flew	flown	fliegen
forget	forgot	forgotten	vergessen
go	went	gone	gehen
get	got	got / AE gotten	bekommen, erhalten
grow	grew	grown	wachsen
have	had	had	haben
hear [hɪə(r)]	heard [hɜːd]	heard [hɜːd]	hören
hide	hid	hidden	verstecken
hit	hit	hit	schlagen, aufprallen auf
hold	held	held	halten
hurt	hurt	hurt	verletzen
keep	kept	kept	behalten
know	knew	known	kennen, wissen
lead	led	led	führen
learn	learnt/learned	learnt/learned	lernen
leave	left	left	verlassen
let	let	let	lassen
lose	lost	lost	verlieren
make	made	made	machen
mean	meant	meant	bedeuten
meet	met	met	sich treffen
pay	paid	paid	(be-)zahlen
put	put	put	setzen, stellen, legen
read [riːd]	read [red]	read [red]	lesen
ring	rang	rung	läuten, klingeln, anrufen
rise	rose	risen	steigen
run	ran	run	laufen
say	said	said	sagen
see	saw	seen	sehen
sell	sold	sold	verkaufen
send	sent	sent	senden, schicken
shoot	shot	shot	(er-)schießen
sing	sang	sung	singen
sit	sat	sat	sitzen
speak	spoke	spoken	sprechen
spend	spent	spent	ausgeben, verbringen (Zeit)
stand	stood	stood	stehen
take	took	taken	nehmen
teach	taught	taught	unterrichten, lehren
tell	told	told	erzählen, mitteilen, sagen
think	thought	thought	denken, meinen
understand	understood	understood	verstehen
wake	woke	woken	wecken
write	wrote	written	schreiben

FOCUS ON GRAMMAR

Arbeitsbuch
zur Wiederholung
zentraler grammatischer
Strukturen

LÖSUNGEN

Cornelsen

Focus on Grammar – Seite 4

1 Adjectives

1a

Greek; golden; brilliant; best; most beautiful; unforgettable; spectacular; most incredible; historical; cultural; lively; wide; local; international; more adventurous; excellent; natural; pleasant

1b

superlative: best, most beautiful, most incredible; comparative: more adventurous

2

1 better, best; **2** more incredible, most incredible; **3** more beautiful, most beautiful; **4** quieter, quietest; **5** wider, widest; **6** more pleasant, most pleasant; **7** worse, worst; **8** livelier; liveliest

Focus on Grammar – Seite 5

3

1 consistently; **2** fully, privately, particular; **3** inclusive, normally; **4** well, local; **5** different, regularly; **6** extremely, easy, fully

4

1 more comfortable than, the most comfortable; **2** as expensive as, less expensive; **3** nearest, nearer, than; **4** bigger, as big as, most

5

1 wider, than; **2** warm, as; **3** public; **4** lovely; **5** attractive, than; **6** hottest; **7** easier, than; **8** normal; **9** great; **10** important, than

6

1. The Hilton hotel is the biggest and most modern hotel in the city.
2. The wine smells and tastes good.
3. A holiday in England is more expensive than a holiday in Germany.
4. The weather in Spain was worse than at home.
5. A holiday in a hotel is not as adventurous as a holiday in a tent.

Focus on Grammar – Seite 6

2 Adverbs

1a

definitely (think); brilliantly (works); exactly (leads); accurately (showed); amazingly (whole sentence); quickly (recognizes); really (don't have to read); intuitively (work it out); outstandingly (well); well (navigates); thoroughly (recommend)

1b

outstandingly

1c

Amazingly

2

1	accurately	more accurately	most accurately	accurate
2	badly	worse	worst	bad
3	easily	more easily	most easily	easy
4	angrily	more angrily	most angrily	angry
5	well	better	best	good
6	fast	faster	fastest	fast
7	expensively	more expensively	most expensively	expensive
8	hard	harder	hardest	hard

Focus on Grammar – Seite 7

3

1 well; **2** actually; **3** seriously; **4** usually; **5** slowly; **6** badly; **7** easily; **8** Unfortunately

4

1 fantastic; **2** extremely; **3** excellent; **4** unfortunately; **5** seriously; **6** definitely; **7** light; **8** dead; **9** especially; **10** good

5

1. Expensive navigation systems work more accurately than cheap navigation systems. / Cheap navigation systems do not work as accurately as expensive navigation systems.
2. The Transrapid runs faster than high speed trains. / High speed trains do not run as fast as the Transrapid.
3. Most young people understand technology better than old people. / Old people do not understand technology as well as most young people.

6

1 a very well built car; 2 a classically designed camera;
3 extremely user-friendly software; 4 a surprisingly low price; 5 a disappointingly small screen

7

2 late; 3 nearly; 4 wide; 5 hardly; 6 mostly;
7 closely; 8 lately; 9 highly; 10 dangerously

Focus on Grammar – Seite 8

3 Word order

1

2 But this number rises to about 50,000 every summer.
3 Young people go there to enjoy the pubs and parties from June to August.
4 The first teenage alcoholics appeared in Tenby a few years ago.
5 Obviously most pub owners don't allow young people to drink in their pub.
6 Unfortunately it does happen now and again.
7 The police sometimes close pubs where young people are served alcohol.
8 So any teenagers who are under 18 years old are mostly not served.
9 Young people usually drink too much because of peer pressure.
10 Binge drinking has already become a huge problem in Britain.

Focus on Grammar – Seite 9

2

2 Tenby depends completely on thousands of tourists and it is hardly interested in a few local teenagers.
3 Society says young people should enjoy themselves in clubs and bars at the weekend.
4 The owner of the pub near us will only serve us kids in the winter – when the tourists have gone.
5 It can definitely be a problem even if you're not underage. If you look young, you have to show ID in some bars.
6 Bars are not just for getting drunk in, you know – my friends and I are happy to sit and drink peacefully in a corner.
7 I'd say that the police haven't managed the situation sensibly in Tenby so far.
8 There are lots of bars where they check your ID at the door.
9 My boyfriend and his friends are generally drunk by ten o'clock at night.

3

2 ✗ But we Germans also …
3 ✗ … but they generally don't … at the pub in the evening
4 ✗ … drunk teenagers in the town centre after midnight.
5 ✗ … I have frequently seen violence.
6 ✗ … and they often stay like that …
7 ✓
8 ✗ … my school friends regularly drink …
9 ✓
10 ✗ Maybe they will become …

4

1 Too much alcohol can completely destroy the brain.
2 The problem is hardly solvable.
3 Unfortunately many teenagers regularly drink spirits.
4 Young girls also drink in pubs and discos at the weekend.
5 Youths who are often drunk are mostly aggressive.
6 Alcohol is the cause of violence on the streets again and again.
7 You seldom saw anti-social behaviour in Great Britain a few years ago.
8 The situation has generally got out of control in some cities.

Focus on Grammar – Seite 10

4 Quantifiers A

1

1 some; 2 any, 3 some; 4 some; 5 any; 6 some; 7 some; 8 any; 9 any; 10 some; 11 some; 12 some; 13 any

Focus on Grammar – Seite 11

2

1 some, something; 2 anybody, anything; 3 anywhere; 4 somebody, somewhere; 5 any

3

1 Each; 2 every, every; 3 Each/Every; 4 each; 5 every

4

1 each; 2 everybody; 3 everywhere; 4 everything; 5 everybody; 6 every; 7 everybody

5

1 None; 2 nothing; 3 nowhere; 4 Nobody; 5 nothing

Focus on Grammar – Seite 12

5 Quantifiers B

1

1 many / a lot of; 2 few; 3 little; 4 a little; 5 less; 6 little;
7 much; 8 less; 9 many / a lot of; 10 fewer; 11 fewer;
12 many; 13 many; 14 much; 15 little; 16 many / a lot of;
17 fewer; 18 less

Focus on Grammar – Seite 13

2

1 a little; 2 a lot of / many; 3 few; 4 a few; 5 less; 6 most;
7 little; 8 a few; 9 many / a lot of; 10 a few; 11 less;
12 fewer

3

1 None of us can be happy all the time.
2 Not everybody is able to define happiness.
3 This institute does a survey every two years or so.
4 I cannot imagine any method at all that might improve things for us.
5 Fewer kids appear to be happy in today's world.
6 Most youngsters need rules and guidance to help them find a path to happiness.
7 How many of us here would be interested in going to the CP centre?
8 There seems to be little hope of arranging a visit at the moment.

4

1 None of the young people thought that a Labrador would help much.
2 Fewer worries mean that you are less unhappy.
3 Most women who are unhappy are often a little more depressed up to 30 or 40 than men of the same age.
4 Many older people are quite happy most of the time.
5 None of us is always balanced because everybody has some negative feelings.
6 Each of the kids has learnt something from the CP program.
7 It can happen to anybody at any time.
8 There are happy people somewhere in this world.

Focus on Grammar – Seite 14

Focus on ... Prepositional verbs

1

2 look in sth = in etw hineinschauen, laugh at sth = über etw lachen
3 agree on sth = sich auf etw einigen
4 depend on sth = von etw abhängen
5 belong to sb = jdm gehören, believe in sth = glauben an etwas
6 live on sth = von etw leben; die for sth = für etw sterben

2

1 agree on; 2 believe in; 3 rely on; 4 depends on,
5 belong to; 6 live on

3

1 i; 2 b; 3 l; 4 j; 5 d; 6 c; 7 k; 8 e; 9 h; 10 f; 11 g; 12 a

Focus on Grammar – Seite 15

Test 1

1

1 comfortable; 2 fast, quiet; 3 hardly, terribly, loud;
4 surprisingly, low

2

1 better at French than; 2 as good as; 3 the best; 4 the least successful; 5 as successful as Peter; 6 most successful

3

1 Sheila often has to work in the hospital at night.
2 The patients sometimes give her a hard time.
3 Yesterday a patient called her to come to his room three times after midnight.
4 She usually goes home at 6 a.m. after a night shift.
5 Her husband often only sees her at dinner.

4

1 anybody; 2 anywhere, Each, somebody;
3 Some, any; nowhere; 4 every, everything

5

1 many, many; 2 a lot of, much; 3 less; 4 few; 5 fewer

Focus on Grammar – Seite 16

6 Present tenses

1a

simple present: It's, there are, It sometimes feels, it doesn't really bother, everybody wants, I come from, They ask, My host family is, My host mom knows, I can join, I share, She's, we get along, I often miss, I don't feel lonely, I really miss, There's nothing, that's; present continuous: I'm doing here

1b

a

2

1 shares; **2** doesn't feel; **3** misses; **4** likes; **5** doesn't phone

3

1 There are a lot of Latinos in Marion's school.

Focus on Grammar – Seite 17

2 Most students want to talk to her.
3 Marion and Avril share a room.
4 Marion's host mum knows the basketball trainer.
5 Marion misses her family.
6 Marion doesn't feel lonely.

4

1 Who comes home from school at 3 o'clock?
2 What does she miss?
3 Who shares the room?
4 Who does Marion get along with very well?
5 Who does Marion phone every week?

5

1 are you doing; **2** am writing; **3** am watching; **4** are showing; **5** is cooking; **6** am just leaving

6

1 listens, takes, is still sleeping, is dreaming; **2** starts, is getting up; **3** has, is going, go; **4** has, eats, doesn't like, is having, is enjoying

7

1 F; **2** D; **3** E; **4** A; **5** B; **6** C

8

1 What is he doing? – He's writing a letter.
2 Who pays for the costs of the exchange?
3 How do you find a good American school?
4 What interests German students in America?
5 More and more exchange students are coming to America.
6 Some students don't get on well with their host parents.

Focus on Grammar – Seite 18

7 Past tenses A

1a

1 saw; **2** were; **3** bought; **4** showed; **5** recognized; **6** knew; **7** called; **8** told; **9** had; **10** didn't even have; **11** didn't know; **12** developed; **13** worked; **14** left; **15** started; **16** became

Focus on Grammar – Seite 19

b

Paul Allen was reading

1c

b

2

Across: **1** slept; **3** blew; **5** redid; **7** drank; **8** cut; **11** sped; **12** began; **13** thought; **15** held; **16** stood
Down: **1** struck; **2** paid; **3** bound; **4** won; **6** drew; **9** taught; **10** dreamt; **11** sought; **12** bit; **14** had

3

1 Where did Bill's friend first see the picture of Altair?
2 Where did Bill study?
3 Did it take long to develop the program?
4 Did the program work when they demonstrated it?
5 Which computer did they use to develop BASIC?

4

1 Who helped to develop the MS-DOS system?
2 What did Bill's parents leave him?
3 What fascinated Bill in his early youth?
4 What did Bill study at Harvard?
5 What did Paul show Bill one day?
6 Who developed BASIC?

5

1 were working, called; **2** were already waiting, was first sold; **3** came out, were debating; **4** was looking for, was launched

6

1 When Microsoft started to sell Windows Vista, Windows XP had been on the market for nearly six years.
2 Bill Gates had been the leading person in Microsoft for 25 years when he decided to withdraw from the day to day business in the company.

Focus on Grammar – Seite **20**

3 Many computer manufacturers and business customers had tried out Windows Vista before Microsoft released the program worldwide.
4 Many customers who had used Windows XP were very excited when they heard about Vista.
5 Microsoft had spent an enormous amount of money on the development of Vista but they were pleased with the result.

7

1 had been working, sold; **2** had been interviewing, got; **3** formed, had been donating; **4** had only been using, decided; **5** started, had been studying

8

1 After he had left Harvard, Bill founded Microsoft.
2 What had Bill been doing all the years before he studied at Harvard?
3 I was playing a game when the computer broke down.
4 I couldn't remember where I had put my laptop so I used the computer instead.
5 I had never forgotten to switch my computer off before.

9

1 tried to, took; **2** had been, turned itself off, **3** had been typing, disappeared; **4** had been surfing, froze

Focus on Grammar – Seite **21**

5 put, didn't want, had brought, was working, heard, had forgotten

10

1 I hadn't heard about Windows Vista until I saw an article about it in the paper.
2 I didn't buy a new computer last year.
3 When I was young, I wanted to be a computer expert.
4 Richtig.
5 I had been using Windows XP for two years when I bought a computer with Vista.

11

1 was studying, b; **2** did Microsoft release, b; **3** had Microsoft launched, c; **4** had been working, c; **5** were, a

Focus on Grammar – Seite **22**

8 Past tenses B

1

1 has just come in; **2** has erupted; **3** has not caused; **4** has since reached; **5** has been; **6** has finally started; **7** has not been; **8** have described

Focus on Grammar – Seite **23**

2

1 The Stromboli volcano has become well-known in recent years.
2 Etna has also attracted lots of attention over the decades.
3 Experts have always considered Etna to be the more dangerous of the two volcanoes.
4 They have still not decided if Etna might erupt soon.
5 There has not been a major catastrophe on Sicily yet.
6 Have you ever experienced an eruption first hand? – No, but I've seen the damage afterwards.

3

1 have been; **2** happened; **3** destroyed; **4** pushed; **5** moved; **6** still haven't forgotten; **7** broke out; **8** burned; **9** died; **10** lost; **11** were forced; **12** have recently shown

4

K	L	A	S	T	J	O	N	B	E	Y
V	J	S	T	I	L	L	O	E	A	Z
E	I	A	L	L	B	R	A	D	N	M
V	C	L	B	N	W	N	R	F	A	O
E	A	A	R	E	C	E	N	T	L	Y
R	L	T	Q	K	T	E	D	O	W	U
H	E	E	U	S	W	H	E	N	A	G
Y	R	L	E	C	A	X	D	G	Y	F
M	I	Y	H	P	G	E	J	U	S	T
S	T	U	R	T	O	N	S	W	T	Y

present perfect: since, ever, always, still, lately, just, recently, yet; simple past: last, when, yesterday, ago

Focus on Grammar – Seite **24**

5

1 Etna hasn't erupted recently.
2 The San Andreas Fault has moved several metres over 100 years.

3 Several earthquakes have occurred in California lately.
4 Since about 1995 there have been more hurricanes than usual in the Gulf of Mexico.
5 The volcano hasn't erupted yet.
6 The German city of Freiburg was hit by some small quakes last year.
7 In the 1906 earthquake about 300,000 were made homeless.
8 The city hasn't had any earthquakes up to now.

6

1 For; 2 Since; 3 since; 4 for; 5 for; 6 since

7

1 b, a; 2 a, b; 3 b, a; 4 a, b; 5 b, a; 6 a, b

8

1 have known; 2 have just succeeded; 3 have been living; 4 have been killed; 5 have lost; 6 has been working; 7 has just laid; 8 has the world been dreaming

Focus on Grammar – Seite 25

9

2 Dr Smith has been researching tsunamis for years.
3 The volcano has been active since 1645.
4 San Francisco hasn't had a major earthquake since 1906.
5 I have been interested in earthquakes since I was a child.
6 The US has been making tsunami buoys for a few years.

10a

1 Etna has been active for centuries.
2 A lot of people have died in tsunamis recently.
3 About 200, 000 people died in December 2004.
4 The volcano hasn't erupted yet.
5 They have been talking about the new buoy all day.
6 There was a big earthquake 12 hours ago.
7 The hurricane has been blowing for two days.
8 The tsunami victims have been waiting for help for weeks.
9 The 1906 earthquake in San Francisco started at 5 a.m.

10b

10 Stuart schreibt seit zwei Jahren an einem Buch über Vulkane.
11 Seit der Stromboli letzten Monat ausgebrochen ist gab es zwei Flutwellen.
12 Seitdem das neue Warnsystem entwickelt wurde, sind weniger Leute gestorben.
13 Die Leute in San Francisco warten schon seit Jahrzehnten auf das nächste große Erdbeben.

11

1 caused, c; 2 has erupted, destroyed, a; 3 hasn't erupted, exploded, c; 4 has experienced, was, b; 5 caused, b

Focus on Grammar – Seite 26

9 Future tenses

1

1 F; 2 A; 3 E; 4 C; 5 D; 6 B

2

P	S	F	S	U	P	P	O	S	E
R	B	E	L	I	E	V	E	I	R
O	R	T	J	L	P	P	H	M	V
B	O	M	A	Y	B	E	O	A	T
A	S	S	U	M	E	R	P	G	H
B	W	H	D	C	B	H	E	I	I
L	A	W	B	R	T	A	T	N	N
Y	Y	S	T	O	N	P	U	E	K
F	O	R	E	C	A	S	T	T	J
A	Q	H	O	P	D	B	N	R	T

Focus on Grammar – Seite 27

3

1 will be; 2 will develop; 3 will have to; 4 will vanish; 5 will move; 6 will reduce; 7 are not going to build; 8 are going to close; 9 won't manage; 10 will be able to; 11 will start; 12 will invest; 13 will mean; 14 won't lead; 15 won't give; 16 will cause

4

1 I don't think the UK will ever introduce the Euro.
2 The company is going to build a new factory in India next year.
3 The EU will probably expand to include some new members.
4 More people will lose their jobs with more companies outsourcing.
5 It is clear that more people will move within the EU in the future.
6 Experts think the Euro will become a strong currency.

5

1 is building; 2 starts; 3 gets; 4 have; 5 is advertising; 6 are reducing; 7 are not increasing; 8 are being made; 9 is ending; 10 remain

Focus on Grammar – Seite 28

6

1 **1** will enjoy; **2** will have
2 **1** will be; **2** takes; **3** won't have
3 **1** am selling; **2** plan; **3** will give up
4 **1** are you emigrating; **2** are you going to do; **3** will vanish; **4** am leaving; **5** starts
5 **1** will improve; **2** are increasing; **3** will do; **4** will probably try

Focus on Grammar – Seite 29

7

1 will have trained/will be training; **2** will be taking place/will have taken place; **3** will have improved; **4** will have learned; **5** will have become; **6** won't be putting

8

1 It is obvious that I won't get the new job in Manchester.
2 We hope there will be a minimum wage in the EU.
3 Once our country is a member of the EU, our salaries will rise.
4 I'm going to work/I will be working in Madrid next month.
5 The train leaves this morning at 10.
6 We are opening a subsidiary in Tallinn this spring.
7 He will have sold his flat by the end of the week.
8 He is planning to give up his job at Christmas.
9 I can't find the documents. – I'll look for them then.
10 When will Turkey have joined the EU by?

9

1 I assume production won't start soon.
2 We probably won't finish the design work for another six months or so.
3 Richtig.
4 We forecast that the market for small aircraft in India will increase by 25%.
5 We need more time on the engine design before Delhi Air decides on a price.
6 As soon as I have more information, I can email you again with the final details.

Focus on Grammar – Seite 30

10 The passive

1

is used to, is thought, were used by, was taken, were later found, be ignored, is thought, could be caused by, have not been proven

2

1 is limited; **2** be achieved; **3** have been used; **4** are taken; **5** were asked; **6** are often punished; **7** was taken away

Focus on Grammar – Seite 31

3

2 Steroids have been used by athletes for years./Steroide werden seit Jahren von Athleten benutzt.
3 Steroids can be detected months after they have been taken./Steroide können noch Monate nachdem sie eingenommen wurden nachgewiesen werden.
4 Steroids cannot be bought legally./Steroide können nicht legal gekauft werden.
5 The use of steroids is banned in all major sports./Die Einnahme von Steroiden ist in allen großen Sportarten verboten.
6 The side effects of steroids are still felt/will still be felt in later life./Die Nebenwirkungen von Steroiden sind noch im späteren im Leben zu spüren.

4

2 were taken away; **3** are being developed; **4** will be tested; **5** gave; **6** have appeared

5

1 He was given an unknown drug.
2 She was not allowed to use steroids.
3 I was asked if I had ever taken drugs.
4 Some steroids were found in the athlete's bag.
5 The drugs were bought illegally on the black market.

6

1 It is said that drugs don't help in all sports.
2 It has been thought for a long time that drugs and crime are linked.
3 It is known that taking drugs is dangerous but this doesn't stop a lot of people.
4 It has always been suspected that drugs change the drug user's personality.

7

1 Some drugs were stolen last week.
2 The thief hasn't been caught yet.
3 We hope he will be arrested soon.
4 He may be sent to prison.

8

1 has been discovered; **2** are usually bought; **3** was analysed; **4** is believed, will be used, cannot be detected/discovered; **5** were explained to him by

Focus on Grammar – Seite 32

Focus on... False friends and other problems

Quiz A

wrong sentences: **1**, **3**, **5**, **6**, **8**, **9**, **10**, **12**, **14**, **16**, **18**, **21**, **23**

Focus on Grammar – Seite 33

9

1 your opinion; **2** The meaning; **3** Our grammar school, gymnasium; **4** a sensible idea; **5** Actually, current; **6** The actual danger; **7** get, university/college; **8** a high school; **9** a good, very sensitive boy; **10** to work in a laboratory; **11** a small guest house, her pension; **12** brave; likeable; **13** consistent; **14** old alleys and elegant avenues

2

1. Every Christian believes in Christ.
2. The current advertising campaign will be expensive.
3. Who's the boss of this company?
4. She acted consistently – that's why she's been successful.
5. Richtig.
6. We design PCs in our laboratory.
7. Richtig.
8. Richtig.

Quiz B

Wrong sentences: **1**, **3**, **4**, **5**, **6**, **9**, **10**, **12**, **13**, **14**, **15**, **17**, **18**, **20**

Focus on Grammar – Seite 34

3

1 damage has; **2** My binoculars are lying; **3** His knowledge of French was; **4** A good piece of advice helps; **5** Your good advice was; **6** is, news; **7** No news is good news; **8** The USA possesses; **9** Most people enjoy; **10** The goods weigh 200 kilos; **11** Politics is; **12** Some new information has

Focus on Grammar – Seite 35

Test 2

1

1. I like to go to discos at the weekend.
2. What are you doing? – I'm reading a book.
3. Today is Saturday and I'm playing football. I normally only play on Fridays.

2

1 got, was sitting; **2** hadn't started, gave; **3** worked, was sitting, didn't have, was; **4** appeared, had already published; **5** raised, was filming, bought

3

1 hasn't the government done; **2** tried; **3** has been cooperating; **4** have improved; **5** have not invested; **6** have been hoping; **7** haven't had enough

4

1 will be swimming; **2** will be; **3** leaves; **4** won't buy; **5** will have been

5

1. 20 years ago computers were mostly used in offices.
2. Today more home computers are bought than office ones.
3. Work has been greatly changed by computers.

Focus on Grammar – Seite 36

11 Reported speech

1

1 had made; **2** had been; **3** was, **4** was; **5** could learn; **6** couldn't find; **7** had; **8** felt; **9** saw; **10** had always had; **11** accepted

Focus on Grammar – Seite 37

2

1. what the government had done to help immigrants with immigration.
2. if the economy would get weaker with so many immigrants.
3. if immigrants would lose their cultural identify if they adjusted to 'British' culture.

4 what the advantages of having immigrants were.
5 if immigrants should learn the English language.
6 why British people didn't try to make it easier for foreigners to integrate.

3

1 must improve; 2 not only talk; 3 advised me to try to understand; 4 told me not to break; 5 to try to find

4

1 had got; 2 that day; 3 had lost his; 4 the week before; 5 would call; 6 the next day if he got the job

5

1 Achmed told me that he had lost his job.
2 Zara said she wanted / Zara says she wants to move to Britain.
3 Richtig.
4 He said he had read a report about immigration in his local paper the week before.
5 Richtig.

Focus on Grammar – Seite **38**

12 Modal auxiliaries A

1

1	2	3	4	5	6	7	8	9	10	11
r	e	p	l	a	c	e	m	e	n	t

Focus on Grammar – Seite **39**

2

1 aren't allowed to, will be able/allowed to; 2 be allowed to, are allowed to; 3 has been able/allowed to, can / are able to; 4 can't, will be able to; 5 can't / aren't / haven't been / able to, will be able to; 6 are allowed to, not be allowed to; 7 be allowed to

3

2 May I ask you some questions about your religion?
3 Robots aren't able to think yet.
4 You aren't allowed to smoke in German restaurants.
6 I wasn't able to understand what he said.

4

1 In the future cars will be able to fly.
2 When the scientists created the robot, he was able to make simple decisions.
3 The doctor couldn't / wasn't able to cure his patient.

4 The computer was very powerful but it wasn't able to answer the question.
5 In 1969 the spacecraft Apollo 11 was able to travel to the moon.
6 Many authors have written stories about what we will be able to do in the future.
7 Richtig.
8 Richtig.

5

1 In the past children weren't allowed to disagree with / contradict their parents.
2 Were you allowed to smoke at home?
3 Will we be able to stop global warming?
4 Robots have been able to put car parts together for many years.
5 You/it shouldn't be allowed to manufacture/create embryos from stem cells.
6 May I ask you a few questions about stem cell research?
7 Should scientists be able to clone humans?

Focus on Grammar – Seite **40**

13 Modal auxiliaries B

1

1 must; 2 needn't; 3 must; 4 mustn't; 5 needn't; 6 must; 7 needn't

2

1 might be cheaper than travelling to America.
2 might be worse than it is here.
3 The guide might have given us the wrong information.
4 We might have to wait a long time for the next train.

Focus on Grammar – Seite **41**

3

1 did you have to; 2 had to; 3 had to; 4 Did you have to; 5 didn't have to; 6 have never had to; 7 have to; 8 had to; 9 don't have to; 10 will have to

4

1 should; 2 needn't; 3 should; 4 mustn't; 5 should; 6 should; 7 should; 8 needn't

5

1 used to; 2 didn't use to; 3 used to; 4 didn't use to; 5 used to

6

1	2	3	4	5	6	7
l	i	c	e	n	c	e

7

1 In some countries foreign drivers must have an international driving licence.
2 You are allowed to smoke in German restaurants.
3 Germans had to have a visa to visit the US in the past.
4 You needn't / don't have to be at the airport for longer than two hours before the departure of international flights.
5 Why did you have to fly on Sunday?

Focus on Grammar – Seite 42

14 If-clauses

1

1 decides, will not make; 2 increase, will rise; 3 melts, will cause; 4 will prefer, rises; 5 starts, will be able to; 6 will be, stay

2

1 are able to; 2 has to; 3 start; 4 can; 5 travel; 6 cause; 7 take; 8 walk; 9 help; 10 are: 11 fly; 12 are; 13 take; 14 reduce

Focus on Grammar – Seite 43

3

1 You would think of the Sahara if you saw some parts of China today.
2 If I were a world leader, I would do something about climate change right now.
3 I could buy an environmentally-friendly car if I earned more money.
4 If we all used less energy, we might be able to stop further environmental damage.
5 We would create less rubbish if we recycled more.
6 The air would be much cleaner if we didn't fly so much.

4

1 hadn't doubled, wouldn't have put up; 2 wouldn't have been hit, had remained; 3 hadn't changed, wouldn't have disappeared; 4 would be, had been built, we had introduced; 5 had burned, might have meant

5

2 if we don't protect the atmosphere. (Type 1)
3 If the ice melts in Greenland, (Type 1)
4 if we hadn't produced as much CO_2. (Type 3)
5 if we did something about global warming straightaway. (Type 2)
6 if animals and plants die. (Type 1)

6

1 If we don't do anything soon, it will be too late to stop climate change.
2 If we use our cars less, we will cause less pollution.
3 We would go on holiday in Scandinavia if it were warmer there.
4 If I were you, I would buy a hybrid car.
5 Sylt could have been flooded if sea levels had risen dramatically.
6 If the government had had enough money, they would have done more for the environment last year.

Focus on Grammar – Seite 44

15 Relative clauses

1

1 who; 2 which; 3 who; 4 which; 5 which

2

1 who/that; 2 which/that; 3 not necessary; 4 not necessary; 5 which/that; 6 whose; 7 whose; 8 not necessary; 9 that; 10 which/that

Focus on Grammar – Seite 45

3

1 which
2 not necessary
3 , which
4 Doctors, many of whom … for years,
5 which
6 , whose … affected,
7 , who
8 , whose … small,
9 , who
10 who … dangers,

4

1 Foundation, which ... company, ...
2 company, whose ... USA, ... Africa, which ...
3 that/which ... whose
4 which
5 which
6 members, without whom ... little, ...

5a

1 AIDS is a disease whose origin we know.
2 It is a problem which can destroy our society.
3 We have to do all (that) we can.
4 Many young people, whom doctors talk to, don't understand the danger.
5 The foundation, which has spent a lot of money on orphans, has helped a lot.
6 Everyone knows (that) sex without using a condom is stupid.

Contact clauses: **3**, **4**, **6**

5b

1 Die Projekte, die wir finanzieren, sind alle in Afrika.
2 Viele der Patienten, die sie behandeln, sind Kinder.
3 Die Organisation, für die Peter arbeitet, ist in Kenia.
4 Der Kondom, das man in seiner Tasche hat, könnte dasjenige sein, das man braucht, um sein Leben zu retten.

Focus on Grammar – Seite 46

Focus on ... Spelling A

Quiz A

Wrong sentences: **1**, **3**, **4**, **5**, **6**, **8**, **10**, **12**, **13**, **14**, **15**, **18**

1

1 ✗ They were robbed ...
2 ✗ The firm is offering ...
3 ✗ ... the new dress fitted her.
4 ✓
5 ✗ If you don't stop quarrelling, ...
6 ✗ ... he preferred Greece.
7 ✓
8 ✗ We're developing ...

Focus on Grammar – Seite 47

Test 3

1

1 If Ms Jones had had a bit more experience, we would have offered her the job immediately.
2 If the firm gives her a position, she will have to phone lots of clients in Spain.
3 Ms Jones would also work in our office in Madrid if she spoke Spanish.
4 If we paid for a Spanish course, I think Ms Jones would learn the language in no time.
5 I'm sure she will be a great secretary if we give her the job.

2

1 was; **2** their; **3** had been chosen; **4** would bring; **5** their; **6** would create; **7** did not get; **8** there; **9** would change

3

1 which/that; **2** who/that; **3** who; **4** who/that; **5** whose

4

1 shouldn't/mustn't; **2** can; **3** can; **4** have to; **5** don't have to; **6** shouldn't / don't have to; **7** can

Focus on Grammar – Seite 48

16 The participle

1

3 When first introduced ... fair trade products ...;
4 If offered ... a coffee grower in Peru ...;
5 given; 6 Becoming ... rich countries;

Focus on Grammar – Seite 49

7 until helped; **8** After running

2

2 Fair trade products sold well in Britain last year, increasing sales by 48%.
3 Fair trade offers a small profit for good work, aiming to help the poor.
4 The fair trade system covers many types of product, including clothes and furniture.
5 Footballs made in Africa are also part of the fair trade system, costing around £40 rather than the usual £30.
6 The Fairtrade foundation clearly marks its products, using its logo as a label.

7 Many people organise their own events, promoting fair trade in schools and local communities.
8 More and more people recognize the Fairtrade label, proving the foundation is raising awareness about trade.

3

1 With York being famous for its chocolate
2 With the number of chocolate fans in Britain growing bigger and bigger
3 With Dr Sentamu having so many supporters now
4 With companies not wanting to lose customers nowadays
5 with so many poor workers needing money

4

1 Before buying the coffee, the customer asked about the fair trade symbol.
2 While living in Nigeria, she worked for Fair Deal Footballs.
3 'That's very expensive,' he said, pointing to the tea.
4 With so much fair trade chocolate being eaten nowadays, many families in Ghana are earning more money than before.
5 The West is trying to help Africa, hoping to find new customers.
6 If produced in Asia, it will be very cheap.

Focus on Grammar – Seite **50**

17 Forms of ‚lassen'

1

1 not allow people to starve; **2** not let our government forget; **3** permit politicians to spend; **4** let them do; **5** allows children to die; **6** don't permit them to live; **7** let the BBC broadcast; **8** let the world continue; **9** allow a continent to stay; **10** let music change

Focus on Grammar – Seite **51**

2

1 The G8 countries must be made to increase their aid.
2 How do you make them understand their obligations?
3 Years ago it made me cry to see how little they did but now it makes me smile to see things are a little better at last.
4 If the G8 members are not made to realize how terrible the problem is, then the world is lost.
5 We should feel ashamed that we have not made Africans stop dying on our TV screens!
6 If politicians aren't made to show respect for the weak, then there's no future for any of us.

3

1 had ten concerts organised; **2** have international policy changed; **3** had a stage put up; **4** had white wristbands produced; **5** having £28.8 billion pounds allocated

4

1 The G8 countries were made to act quickly.
2 Why do we let people starve?
3 The situation made me cry.
4 We have to make the West donate more.
5 Geldof had the rich nations give more aid.
6 He will have some new concerts organised.
7 How can you make the world change old ideas?

5

1 Geldof and his friend Midge Ure made governments take action.
2 The rich world shouldn't let Africans die without trying to help them.
3 Richtig.
4 He had the stadium cleaned directly after the concert.
5 You won't get people to act differently unless you do something.

Focus on Grammar – Seite **52**

18 Gerund

1

1 working; **2** sending off; **3** trying; **4** living; **5** travelling; **6** designing; **7** selling; **8** losing
with infinitive: began (2), started (7)

2

2 being scared about moving to India at first

Focus on Grammar – Seite **53**

3 having Hindi classes last Thursday; **4** thinking about moving back to Britain; **5** working for himself to working for someone else; **6** starting a second business soon

3

1 in improving; **2** of attending; **3** at solving; **4** of listening; **5** on contacting; **6** in doing; **7** from failing; **8** on becoming

4

1 There's no denying; 2 There's no point trying;
3 it's worth looking for; 4 feel like working; 5 it's fun developing; 6 There's no knowing

5

1 Many rich nations are busy investing abroad.
2 Some people dislike having to live in a globalized world.
3 Nowadays everybody is used to buying goods from abroad.
4 I'd suggest trying your luck in India.
5 Is it really worth getting a tutor from Bangalore?
6 I'm thinking of learning maths by e-tutoring.
7 Sue isn't good at making a good impression at interviews.
8 Our family could never imagine leaving Britain for India.

6

1 Consumers in the USA were warned against buying toys from China.
2 Some US firms specialize in importing such products.
3 Is there the possibility of producing them, in Europe?
4 Parents must prevent their children from using such toys.
5 Many parents insist on getting their money back.
6 Firms in China are fed up of being criticized.
7 The economy depends on exporting good quality goods.
8 Good quality is the best method of gaining new customers.

Focus on Grammar – Seite 54

19 Gerund and infinitive

1

1 remembers growing up; 2 Remember to eat; 3 haven't forgotten reading; 4 I forgot to buy; 5 go on eating;
6 went on to explain; 7 can't stop living; 8 stopped to eat;
9 is trying to eat; 10 try eating

Focus on Grammar – Seite 55

2

1 Experts consider obesity to be the cause of many illnesses.
2 Teenagers who attempt to go on a diet can't normally keep to it.
3 Richtig.
4 Many girls wish to become slim at any price.
5 People on diets often regret eating unhealthy food.
6 Statistically, young people who eat very small amounts can expect to develop anorexia.
7 Another problem is bulimia, where people more or less refuse to stop eating.
8 Many people with eating disorders don't manage to change their lifestyle and so die young.

3

1 to ban; 2 to introduce; 3 to give; 4 to limit / limiting;
5 controlling; 6 saying

4

2 I've decided to exercise more.
3 I enjoy going to the gym.
4 Jane promised to eat less chocolate.
5 Matt is good at playing football.
6 I can't afford to join a gym.

5

1 Nobody expects you to lose more than 10 kilos.
2 She is used to going to school without breakfast.
3 I would suggest starting a fitness course next week.
4 We would prefer to eat meat than vegetables.
5 He is planning on trying a new diet.
6 I don't feel like getting fatter every day.
7 Will she manage to do without her daily chocolate in the future?
8 I hate to go / going to bed hungry.

Focus on Grammar – Seite 56

20 Question tags

1

1 didn't they; 2 were they; 3 doesn't it; 4 won't they;
5 can we; 6 hasn't it; 7 don't they; 8 isn't there;
9 are there; 10 don't we

2

1 Let's go to the opening ceremony, shall we?
2 We'll see each other at the game next week, won't we?
3 The tickets were really expensive, weren't they?
4 You can't come with us tomorrow, can you?

Focus on Grammar – Seite 57

Focus on ... Spelling B

Quiz A

Wrong sentences; **1**, **2**, **4**, **5**, **7**, **9**, **10**, **11**, **12**, **14**, **16**, **17**, **18**, **20**, **21**, **22**, **24**

1

1 rebels; **2** emigrate, immigrate; **3** career, success

Focus on Grammar – Seite 58

4 assassinated, commit; **5** parallel, straight; **6** whether, belief, proof; **7** fourteen, forty; **8** Jewish, Muslim

2

1 The Chinese televised an anti-British programme.
2 John has no self-confidence in spite of the fact that he's a well-known singer.
3 He's Irish, sixty-five years old and an ex-policeman.
4 People were surprised, even annoyed to hear that sort of advice from the director, but no one realized that he was actually joking.
5 I cannot seriously believe that another ten-mile walk at the weekend will help me to lose more weight, although I certainly need more exercise.
6 You have been chosen to attend the UN conference in Berlin as part of the UK delegation.

Focus on Grammar – Seite 59

3

1 According to the calendar; **2** Two of my colleagues, in a choir; **3** medicine, poisonous; **4** The thief, two cheques; **5** separate tables

4

1 canoe; **2** ceiling; **3** receive; **4** pronunciation; **5** queue; **6** cocoa; **7** niece; **8** employee

5

1 The word is almost unpronounceable.
2 The new assistant is reliable, self-confident and efficient.
3 Carrie is beautiful and successful.
4 Wait until I come.
5 The plan is admirable, but unimaginable. Are you responsible for it?

Focus on Grammar – Seite 60

Test 4

1

2 after making his first CD; **3** With sales figures of his CDs rising quickly; **4** With rap becoming more and more popular; **5** Until discovered by EGT, Johno; **6** If marketed at Christmas, his new CD

2

1 ✗ She had her hair and make-up done by her beautician.
2 ✓
3 ✗ She made the organisers buy her special bottled water.
4 ✗ She wouldn't let anyone talk to her before the concert.
5 ✓

3

2 of buying an environmentally-friendly car; **3** in finding out more about hybrid cars; **4** against getting a car with a sunroof; **5** of buying my friend's old car; **6** about driving my new car for the first time

4

1 doing; **2** dancing; **3** to book; **4** hiring; **5** to invite; **6** to organize; **7** planning; **8** arranging; **9** buying; **10** thinking about / to think about

Focus on Grammar – Seite 61

Phrasal verbs

1 on; **2** forward to; **3** after; **4** up; **5** up; **6** away